Q&A® 4
Wiley Command Reference

WILEY COMMAND REFERENCES are designed for intermediate to advanced users of computer applications. These fast and easy-to-use sourcebooks give you the essential information you need to carry out commands quickly and concisely. Other Wiley Command References include:

Q&A® 4
Wiley Command Reference

Karim Meghji
Dave Reid

John Wiley & Sons, Inc.
New York • Chichester • Brisbane • Toronto • Singapore

Publisher: Katherine Schowalter
Editor: Laura Lewin
Managing Editor: Nana D. Prior
Copy Editor: Shelley Flannery
Composition: Impressions, A Division of Edwards Brothers, Inc.

In recognition of the importance of preserving what has been written, it is a policy of John Wiley & Sons, Inc. to have books of enduring value published in the United States printed on acid-free paper, and we exert our best efforts to that end.

This publication is designed to provide accurate and authoritative information in regard to the subject matter covered. It is sold with the understanding that the publisher is not engaged in rendering legal, accounting, or other professional service. If legal advice or other expert assistance is required, the services of a competent professional person should be sought. FROM A DECLARATION OF PRINCIPLES JOINTLY ADOPTED BY A COMMITTEE OF THE AMERICAN BAR ASSOCIATION AND A COMMITTEE OF PUBLISHERS.

Library of Congress Cataloging-in-Publication Data

Meghji, Karim.
    Q&A 4 Wiley command reference / Karim Meghji, Dave Reid.
      p. cm.
    ISBN 0-471-54264-4 (pbk.)
    1. Data base management. 2. Q&A (Computer program) I. Reid,
Dave. II. Title. III. Title: Q&A 4 command reference.
QA76.9.D3M43 1992
005.369—dc20   91-40027

Printed in the United States of America
10 9 8 7 6 5 4 3 2 1

Special thanks to my parents for showing me that the sky is truly the limit. Thanks to Julie Brightwell and all my friends who were both understanding and supportive while I was writing this book. Finally, thanks to Lisa Vermont for passing this opportunity on to me.

Karim Meghji

I would like to thank my wife, Michelle, for her unending support during the long nights while writing this book. Edgar Martinez, Dave Hem, and Susan Beech also receive honorable mention. I want to thank both Kathy Johnson and Barbara Callisch because each has, in their own special way, been responsible for helping me start this project.

Dave Reid

Contents

Chapter 3   Report   99

Chapter 4   Write   127

Tables

Introduction

If you're looking for an easy-to-use, step-by-step reference for all the commands and operations in Q&A, you've found the right book. *Q&A 4 Wiley Command Reference* contains essential information on all commands, operations, and concepts surrounding Q&A 4.0 including how to create both databases and documents, programming, columnar and cross tab reports, and uses for custom menus.

Who Can Use This Book?

Everyone! Intended for both beginning and experienced users, this book uses simple language to convey even the most advanced operations. From simple operations such as adding data to a database to complicated operations such as creating Custom Menus, all users will find information suited to their uses of Q&A.

Users of this book, regardless of level, should have Q&A installed on a computer, and be somewhat familiar with DOS.

Beginning users will find fundamental information on all commands in a simple, step-by-step format; important information to get the job done. Advanced users will find detailed explanations, and little known tricks in the form of notes, and examples; information to use the wealth of power in Q&A to its fullest extent.

How to Use This Book

Q&A is a modular product by design. In keeping consistent with the different modules of Q&A, this book is separated into eight chapters:

Chapter 1, General—Covers general concepts of the product, including network features of Q&A, font usage, using Q&A menus, and the Q&A help system.

Chapter 2, File—Details the functionality of the database module in Q&A. Information to design a database, add, remove, modify, and print data from the database can be found in this chapter.

Chapter 3, Report—Discusses the module of Q&A that creates summarized or calculated output of data from the database in a columnar or cross tab format.

Chapter 4, Write—Explains the usage of Q&A's integrated word processor to create documents, merge letters, and mailing labels.

Chapter 5, Assistant—Introduces Q&A's Intelligent Assistant and Query Guide, including information on the use and structure of queries for the Artificial Intelligence interface of a database.

Chapter 6, Utilities—Covers operations and commands that globally affect Q&A, such as default pathnames, installed printers, and manipulation of font files.

Chapter 7, Macros and Menus—Outlines Q&A's powerful macro functions. Discusses uses for Q&A's new custom menu feature.

Chapter 8, Programming—Explains "the basics" of programming, and details each programming expression in Q&A with extensive examples.

Each command is broken into the following sections:

Command Name—All commands are headed with their name.

Areas Available—Programming expressions list those areas in which they may be used (i.e., database programming, navigation programming, mail merge programming, etc.).

Description—A simple description of the command for quick recognition of the operation described in the following sections.

Procedure—A step-by-step explanation of using this command or operation, and the implications of each step's actions.

Parameters—Programming expressions list the parameters, and their effect on the expression.

Notes—Additional information for advanced users, detailing information to enhance the basic use of the command.

Examples—Samples of using the command along with explanations of their effect on the product.

Valid Keystrokes—Keystrokes available from the command.

See Also—Cross-references to other commands that may contain similar or helpful information.

Most command names are consistent with the menu selection, option name, or screen title in Q&A. All commands within each chapter are arranged alphabetically for quick and easy access. Commands that cannot be found by name, can be found in the comprehensive index.

1

General

This chapter offers general information about Q&A. It describes the Q&A Main Menu, how to use the menu structure, and how to use the Q&A help system. Additional topics discussed are Q&A's printing options, using fonts in Q&A, and using Q&A on a network.

Command Line Loading Options

Description: These are optional parameters that can be added to the command line when loading Q&A.

Procedure: 1. From the DOS prompt, type QA followed by a space.

2. Type one or more of the options shown in Table 1.1:

Table 1.1. Command Line Options

Option	Description
Screen Options	
-scc	Loads Q&A in color mode. This should be used with color monitors only.
-smm	Loads Q&A in monochrome mode. This can be used on color or monochrome monitors.
-smc	Loads Q&A in monochrome mode. This should be used if you have a PS/2-type machine and are using a monochrome monitor.
-st	Loads Q&A in monochrome mode for use on an LCD type display.
-a	May be used with the options -smc and -st to change the appearance of enhanced text on the screen. You should use this option if you cannot read some of the text on the screen, such as that which has been underlined.

(continued)

Table 1.1.   Command Line Options *(continued)*

Option	Description
-si?	Clears the current Screen Option. This lets Q&A "auto-detect" the monitor type after it has been forced into a mode with one of the other Screen Options.

Memory Options

Option	Description
-v0	Does not allow Q&A to use any expanded memory. This switch has no effect if there is no expanded memory present.
-ym1	Does not allow Q&A to use any upper memory blocks (UMBs). UMBs are the area of memory between 640K and 1 Megabyte.

Macro Options

Option	Description
-al	When followed by a filename, Q&A loads the specified file as the current macro file, instead of QAMACRO.ASC.
-ad	When followed by a filename, Q&A loads the specified file as the default macro file, instead of QAMACRO.ASC. The default macro filename is remembered and automatically loaded each time Q&A is loaded. To clear saved default, use the option -adQAMACRO.ASC.

Miscellaneous Options

Option	Description
-p	When followed by a valid drive and path (e.g., -pC:\QA), Q&A uses the specified subdirectory for storing that user's configuration files. This option is only available when using a multi-user version of Q&A. For more information on this option, see the command, *Q&A on a Network*.
-g	Does not allow Q&A to use a mouse, even if a driver is loaded.
Document Name	The specified document is automatically loaded into the Type/Edit screen in the Write section, and the user is placed on the Type/Edit screen ready to edit the document. If no path is specified, Q&A looks for the document in the default document subdirectory. If no document is found, there is no effect.
Database Name	The specified database becomes the default database the first time the user is prompted for a database name. If no path is specified, Q&A assumes the file is in the default database subdirectory.

Notes: Separate each option with a space.

Q&A normally auto-detects which monitor type you have (i.e., color or monochrome). The Screen Options should only be used if there is some difficulty loading Q&A without one. The Screen Options are saved by Q&A, so after determining which switch is correct for your system, you won't have to use it again.

See Also: *Q&A on a Network* for more information on the -p option.

Define Page

Description: Controls page dimensions, margin settings, and the printed text width. In the File and Report module this command also allows for header and footer information to be entered. In the Write module you can control the page on which the header/footer and the page number begins.

Procedure: 1. Press F8 from any Print Options screen in the File or Report module, or press Ctrl-F6 in the Write module.

2. At the Define Page screen, set these options. The following options appear in all modules:

Page Width—The width of the whole page including the margins.

Page Length—The length of the whole page including the margins.

Left Margin—The distance from the left edge of the page to the left margin.

Right Margin—The distance from the left edge of the page to the right margin.

Top Margin—The distance from the top edge of the page to the top margin.

Bottom Margin—The distance from the bottom edge of the page to the bottom margin.

Characters per Inch—The number of characters to print per inch across the page.

The following options appear in the File and Report module:

Header—Three lines for text that you want to appear at the top of every printed page.

Footer—Three lines for text that you want to appear at the bottom of every printed page.

The following options appear in the Write module:

Begin Header/Footer on Page #—The page number on which to begin the header and the footer.

Begin Page Numbering With Page #—The number with which to begin page numbering. This will be the number on the first page of the document that has a header or footer. The option will only have an effect if a pound sign (#) is included in the header or footer.

3. Press F10 when finished.

Notes: Although the default values are in characters and lines, the page dimensions and margin values can be entered in inches or centimeters. To specify these values in inches, follow the number with a quote mark (''); for centimeters follow the number with the letters cm. All values should be specified identically except the right margin. If you are entering the right margin in inches or centimeters, the value is the distance from the right edge of the page.

The higher the characters per inch setting (cpi), the more characters will print across the page. If your printer does not support the selected cpi, the text will print in the next highest cpi available. This value can be overridden by fonts or other enhancements applied to text.

In the File and Report modules, to place the current date or time in the header or footer, type either @Date or @Time at the location to display the respective value.

In the File and Report modules, to put a page number in the header or footer, type a pound symbol (#) at the location to display the page number.

In the File and Report modules, you can center text in a header by placing it after an exclamation point (!). Text after a second exclamation point on the same line will be aligned to the right margin. To print a literal exclamation point or pound symbol in the header or footer, precede it with a backslash (\\).

In the File and Report modules, the header and footer can be enhanced by pressing Shift-F6, selecting the appropriate enhancement, and highlighting the text to enhance.

Valid
Keystrokes: F2—In the Write module to return to the Print Options

Shift-F6—In the File and Report module to enhance the header and footer

Ctrl-F9—In the File and Report module to assign fonts in the header and footer

F9—In the File and Report module to return to the Print Options

See Also: *Print Options*

Text Enhancements and Fonts Menu for information on using fonts in the header and footer in the File and Report modules.

Edit Header and Footer in the Write Chapter for information on including the page number in the header and footer.

Font Assignments

Description: Assigns up to nine specific fonts for use in enhancing documents, Print Specs, and reports.

Procedure: 1. Once you are at the Font Assignments screen, if the font filename has already been assigned, then skip to step 2. Otherwise, press F6 to display the List of Font Files, and select the appropriate font file for your printer.

2. Highlight the font field that you want to assign or change, and press F6 to display the List of Available Font Descriptions from the current font file.

3. Highlight the desired font and press Enter.

4. If the selected font is a scalable font, you will need to enter a point size (from 1 to 999) for the font.

5. Repeat steps 2–4 for each font you want to assign.

6. Optionally, press F8 to make this screen the default Font Assignments screen for all new documents, reports, and Print Specs.

7. Press F10 to save the Font Assignments screen.

Notes: The Font Assignments screen displays several pieces of information about each font:

Font Name—Displays the font number (1-8) and the name of the font as chosen from the List of Available Font Descriptions.

Abbr.—Displays an abbreviation of the font name. The abbreviation usually contains the point size and any enhancements (b for bold, m for medium, etc.). This abbreviation is what will be displayed on the status line when the font is used (see *Type/Edit* in the Write Chapter for more information).

Point—This is the point size of the font. The letter "E" will appear if the font is an enhancement, such as underline.

Pitch—This is the number of characters that will print per inch on paper. The letter "E" will appear if the font is an enhancement, and the letter "P" will appear if the font is a proportional font.

Comments—Displays comments about the assigned font. The comments can include the name of the printer, or whether the font is a soft font, a cartridge font, or an internal font.

If the Regular Font is a proportional font (it has a "P" in the Pitch column), you should set the Define Page using inch specifications rather than using characters.

You may copy the default Font Assignments screen to the current document, report, or Print Spec by pressing F5 at any time. This will replace all values currently assigned with those found on the default screen.

You may edit the comments or abbreviation of any font by using the *Modify Font File* command (see the Utilities Chapter). You may also create new font descriptions using this command.

**Valid
Keystrokes:**   F5—Copy the default Font Assignments screen

F6—Display a list of available fonts or font files

F8—Make the current screen the default for all new documents, reports, and Print Specs

See Also: *Modify Font File* in Utilities Chapter to create new font descriptions, or edit any of the provided descriptions.

Text Enhancements and Fonts Menu to select and use the assigned fonts.

Type/Edit in the Write Chapter to enhance a document.

Column/Sort Spec in the Report Chapter to enhance a columnar report.

Cross Tab Spec in the Report Chapter to enhance a cross tab report.

Design/Redesign a Spec in the File Chapter to enhance a Print Spec.

Page Preview

Description: Displays printed output to the screen in a graphic mode. Type size, line spacing, and text enhancements are all shown. Different fonts are not shown.

Procedure: 1. From any Print Options screen, set the Page Preview option to YES.

2. After setting all other options, press F10 to print.

3. The output will display exactly as it would on paper. If the document is a merge document, the database information will be included in the preview.

4. When you are finished viewing the preview, press F2 to return to the Print Options screen. If the document is ready to send to the printer, set the Page Preview option to NO and press F10.

Notes: The preview is initially displayed in a full screen
mode. You may zoom in and out, and scroll through
the preview using the following keys:

F—To display the preview in full screen mode.

H—To display the preview in half screen mode.

N—To display the preview in normal screen mode.
Normal mode is approximately the amount of text
visible on the screen, with 80 columns and 25 rows.

2—Displays the preview with facing pages. Facing
pages will put two complete pages on the screen at
one time (even numbered pages are on the right; odd
numbered pages are on the left).

PgUp and PgDn—To scroll up and down the current
page respectively. These only work in half page or
normal modes.

Ctrl PgUp and Ctrl PgDn—To view the previous and
next pages respectively. In facing pages mode, these
will display the previous or next two pages.

Esc—To cancel the preview and return to the operation that began it.

F2—To return to the Print Options screen to make
any changes and reprint.

Since Page Preview uses a graphics mode, you must
have a graphics adapter in your computer. The supported modes are: Hercules, CGA, EGA, VGA,
MVGA, and MDA.

Any graphs, spreadsheets, or other documents included in the current document by the Print Commands, Graph, Spreadsheet, Join, Queue, and
QueueP will be included in the preview.

See Also: *Print Options*

Print Commands in the Write Chapter.

Print Options _____

Description: Specifies where and how you would like to print.

Procedure: 1. In the File module, in addition to the Print Records, and Design/Redesign a Spec command, F2
from any screen at which the record layout is dis-

played (i.e., Add Data, Search/Update, Program Form, Mass Update, Set Initial Values, etc.) will display these options. In the Report module press F10 from the Column/Sort Spec, Derived Columns screen, Cross Tab Spec, Grouping Spec, or Derived Fields screen. In the Write module, press F2 from the Type/Edit screen or select the Print option from the Write Menu.

2. At the Print Options screen set these options. The following options appear in all modules:

Print To—Select the destination for the output— either an "installed printer" (PtrA, PtrB, PtrC, PtrD, PtrE), DISK, or SCREEN.

Page Preview—Preview the output instead of sending it to the selection in the Print To option. If you select YES the output will appear on your monitor in a graphics mode. If you select NO the output will be sent directly to the selection in the Print To option.

Type of Paper Feed—Determine the source for the paper that is used for the output. Select MANUAL if you are hand feeding the paper, CONTINUOUS if you are using fanfold paper or a laser printer with a single bin, or BIN1, BIN2, or BIN3 when using a cut-sheet feeder or laser printer with multiple bins.

Print Offset—A whole number to align the print head with the left edge of the paper. Entering a positive value moves the head to the right, and a negative value moves the head to the left.

Printer Control Codes—Specify printer-dependent codes for controlling special effects on your printer. These codes are sent to the printer before any data is sent.

The following options appear in the File module only:

Number of Copies—Specify the number of copies to print. The limit is 32000.

Print Field Labels—If you select YES the field labels will be printed along with the field con-

tents. If you select NO only the field contents
will be printed.

Number of Records Per Page—Specify the number of database records you would like to fit on
a single page. This number is dependent on the
number of lines for each record, and whether
or not all fields are being printed.

Number of Labels Across—Specify the number of
forms across each sheet being printed.

Print Expanded Fields—If you select YES, all data
which does not fit in the space on the screen
for fields will be printed. If you select NO only
the data that appears on the screen in the fields
will be printed.

The following options appear in the Write module
only:

From Page—Specify the page from which to begin
printing.

To Page—Specify the page at which to end printing.

Number of Copies—Specify the number of copies
to print. The limit is 32000.

Line Spacing—Controls the line spacing of the
printed document. Selecting SINGLE leaves no
blank lines between printed lines. Selecting
DOUBLE leaves one blank line between printed
lines. Selecting ENVELOPE transfers the address from the top left of a letter onto an envelope.

Justify—Controls where the document prints in
relation to the page margins. Selecting YES will
cause the document to be microjustified if supported by your printer. This means that equal
amounts of space will be added between each
word on each line so that the text will touch
both left and right margins. Selecting NO will
cause the document to be aligned with the left
margin leaving the right margin ragged. Selecting SPACE JUSTIFY will cause space characters
to be added between words on each line so

that the text will touch both left and right margins.

Number of Columns—Controls the number of columns to print per page (1–8). On screen, the document always appears as a single column. At print time, the document is formatted such that the text will fit in the number of columns specified. The text will flow down one column, and then continue at the top of the next column.

Name of Merge File—Specifies the name of the database file to use for a mail merge document. See the *Mail Merge* command in the Write Chapter for additional information.

The following options appear in the Report module for columnar reports only:

Print Totals Only—Determines whether both detail information as well as column subcalculations and calculations are printed, as opposed to printing only subcalculations and calculations.

Justify Report Body—Controls where the report body prints in relation to the page margins set.

Line Spacing—Controls the line spacing in a report.

Allow Split Records—Determines whether or not a page break will split a record between two pages. If the record cannot fit onto a single page, this option has no effect. Selecting YES will allow data from a single record to be split onto two separate pages. Selecting NO will push the entire record onto the next page.

The following options appear in the Report module for cross tab reports only:

Show Results As—Controls how to display cross tab calculations. The different options are:

> **NUMBERS**—Displays the results as numeric data.

% **TOTAL**—Displays the results as percentages of the total for all Summary Field data on the report.

% **ROW**—Displays the results as percentages of the total or count for all data in the row.

% **COLUMN**—Displays the results as percentages of the total or count for all data in the column.

NORMAL—Displays the results as an amount above or below 100, where 100 represents the cross tab average.

Justify Report Body—Controls where the report body prints in relation to the page margins set.

Line Spacing—Controls the line spacing in a report.

3. Press F10 to Print.

See Also: *Define Page* for information on setting the page margins, and size.

Install Printer in the Utilities Chapter for information on installing your printer.

Page Preview for information on previewing prior to printing.

Q&A Main Menu _____

Description: Displays selections leading to the major areas of Q&A. Also may display up to six alternate program selections.

Procedure: 1. When first loading Q&A, or returning from one of its submenus, the Q&A Main Menu is displayed.

2. Select from one of the following choices:

File—Displays the File Menu, which allows data to be entered and changed in databases.

Report—Displays the Report Menu, which allows reports, both Cross Tab and Columnar, to be designed and printed.

Write—Displays the Write Menu, which allows documents to be written, saved, and printed.

Assistant—Displays the Assistant Menu, which allows databases to be taught, and questions to be asked using either the Assistant or Query Guide. This fourth option on the Q&A Main Menu may have a name other than Assistant if you have renamed your Assistant.

Utilities—Displays the Utilities Menu, which allows Global Options to be set and printers to be installed.

Exit—Exits Q&A.

Notes: There may be up to six additional options in a column on the right side of the Main Menu. These options are Alternate Program selections; they may execute other DOS programs, or macros.

**Valid
Keystrokes:** F6—Set User ID and Password

Shift-F6—Clear User ID and Password

See Also: *File Chapter*

Write Chapter

Report Chapter

Assistant Chapter

Utilities Chapter

Set Alternate Programs in the Utilities Chapter to install options on the right side of your Q&A Main Menu.

Q&A on a Network

When you run Q&A on a network, several things operate differently.

Personal Path—If several people will be running the same copy of Q&A at the same time, they can each specify a unique location for Q&A to store their user-specific files. These files include the personal dictionary, the macro file, and the configuration file. To specify a personal path, load Q&A with the command line option -p followed by the path. See *Command Line Loading Options* for more information.

Personal Dictionary—When running a spellcheck, words that are not found in the main dictionary are checked in a personal dictionary, called QAPERS.DCT. If the words are not found there, users may choose to add the word to their personal dictionary. If users load Q&A with the -p option, they will each have their own personal dictionary.

Macro File—Users can define and run macros throughout Q&A. If users load Q&A with the -p option, they will each have their own macro files.

Configuration Files—Q&A stores all Global Options, installed printers, Alternate Programs, and other default settings in a file called QA.CFG. If users load Q&A with the -p option, they will each have their own configuration file.

Shared Databases—Multiple users can access the same database at the same time. If two users are trying to edit a record at the same time, the first user will be able to view and edit the record, while the second user will be able only to view the record.

Shared or Exclusive Operations—Many file operations can be performed by several people at the same time. There are, however, some operations that can be performed by only one user at a time, and still others that completely lock all other users out of the file while they are being performed. Table 1.2 describes which operations are in which class.

Table 1.2.   Multi-User Database Operations

Module	Operation
Shared File—Multi-User Operations	
File	Search/Update
	Add Data
	Table View
	Print Records
	Import Data
	Export Data
Report	Print a Report
Assistant	Report printing
	Update a Single Record
	Add Records
Write	Mail Merge
Other	Macros
Shared File—Single-User Operations	
File	Design a Print Spec
	Assign Access Rights
	Save or Retrieve Named Specs
Report	Design a Report

(continued)

Table 1.2.   **Multi-User Database Operations** *(continued)*

Module	Operation
Locked File—Single-User Operations	
File	Redesign a File
	Customize a File
	Copy
	Mass Update
	Post
	Remove
Assistant	Teach Me About Your Database
	Update many records at one time
Query Guide	Teach Query Guide
Utilities	DOS Commands

Network Conflicts—If a user attempts an operation that is not available because another user is working with the database, they will receive a message indicating that the File is in use by <Network ID>. See *Set Global Options* in the Utilities Chapter.

See Also: *Command Line Loading Options* for more information about the -p personal path option.

Set Global Options in the Utilities Chapter to set your <Network ID>.

Spellcheck in the Write Chapter to add words to a personal dictionary.

_____ *Text Enhancements and Fonts Menu*

Description: Displays a menu of available enhancements and fonts that can be used to enhance documents, reports, and Print Specs.

Procedure: Once at the Text Enhancements and Fonts Menu, select the desired enhancement or font from the following options:

Bold—Text with this enhancement prints with a heavier stroke weight, which results in a darker, heavier printed output.

Underline—Underlined text prints with a line below the letters.

Superscript—Text with this enhancement will print slightly above the line.

Subscript—Text with this enhancement will print slightly below the line.

Italics—Italicized text will print with characters that are slanted.

Strikeout—Text with this enhancement will print with a horizontal line through each letter.

Regular—This selection removes all fonts and enhancements from the selected text.

Fonts 1–8—These options will vary depending on which fonts were assigned through the *Font Assignments* command.

Assign Fonts—Assigns specific fonts for the options of Fonts 1–8.

See Also: *Font Assignments* to assign fonts to Fonts 1–8.

User ID and Password Box

Description: Allows a User ID and Password to be entered to allow entry into a password-protected database. Passwords may also be changed from this screen.

Procedure: 1. The first time you access a password-protected database for each session of Q&A, you will be asked for your User ID and Password.

2. Enter your User ID and press Enter.

3. Enter your Password and press Enter. If you entered a valid User ID and Password combination, you will be allowed access to the database, if not, you should restart with step 2.

4. The next time you use this file, or another file for which the same User ID and Password are valid, you will immediately gain access to the file without having to reenter your User ID and Password.

Notes: Optionally, except when entering a Password with F6 at the Main Menu, you may change your Password by pressing F8 from the User ID and Password Box. Enter your User ID and then your old Password, followed by the new Password, then press Enter. This new Password will appear as a string of asterisks (*) on the Access Control screen.

You may set your Password from the Q&A Main Menu by pressing F6 to display the User ID and Password Box.

For added security, you may clear your User ID and Password from memory by pressing Shift-F6 from the Q&A Main Menu. After clearing the passwords, you cannot immediately access files that you entered passwords for earlier; instead you must reenter the User ID and Password.

Valid Keystrokes: F8—Change your Password

See Also: *Assign Access Rights* in the File Chapter to set or change the access rights to a file.

Using Named Specs

Description: You can save and retrieve Duplicate Specs, Merge Specs, Post Specs, Retrieve Specs, Sort Specs, Table View Specs, and Update Specs wherever they appear throughout Q&A.

Procedure:
1. Once at one of the specs available for saving, enter the specifications to be saved.
2. Press Shift-F8 to save the spec. Type a name for the spec, then press Enter.
3. Press F10 to continue with the operation being performed.

Notes: To use a previously saved Named Spec, press Alt-F8. This displays a list of the saved specs of the current type. Select the desired spec and press Enter. If there are no saved specs of this type, you will be notified by mail.

The specs that are available for saving and the commands in which they are used are as follows:

Duplicate Specs—Remove Duplicate Records

Merge Specs—Import Data, Export Data, Copy Selected Records

Post Specs—Post

Retrieve Specs—Retrieve Spec

Sort Specs—Sort Spec

Table View Specs—Table View

Update Specs—Mass Update

**Valid
Keystrokes:**   Alt-F8—List all Named Specs of the current type

Shift-F8—Save the current spec as a Named Spec

2

File

Q&A's data management functions are based on databases created with the File Module. Databases are groups of similar information in a single file.

Simple databases for mailing lists, or complex, customized databases for inventory systems are designed and customized using the commands on the following pages. Data can be added, viewed, or printed.

Commands available in other chapters complement the commands in this chapter by providing functions not available, such as reports, or mail merge capabilities.

Add Data

Menu Path: File I Add Data

Description: Allows information to be manually entered into the fields of a database.

Procedure: 1. Select Add Data from the File Menu.

2. Enter the name of the file you want to add data to and press Enter.

3. When the form is on the screen you can begin entering information into the fields. You may press F6 to add more information into a field than will display on screen. In text and keyword fields you will see the 32K Field Editor, in all other fields you will see a 240-character Expand Field area at the bottom of the screen.

4. When the current record is finished, you can press F10 to save it and continue adding more records.

5. When you have finished the last record you want to edit, press Shift-F10 to save it and exit the file.

Notes: **Date and Time Fields**—Q&A will automatically format date and time values no matter how you enter them (within reason). If you enter "1 3" into a field,

Q&A will know that you mean January 3 of the current year, and it will be displayed in the format selected from the Global Format Options screen. Likewise, time values can be entered in a casual format and Q&A will format it as specified. If ever Q&A cannot recognize what is entered into a time or date field, a warning box appears asking you to confirm the entry.

Delete a Record—If you want to completely remove the current record you can press F3. Answering YES to the warning screen will remove the record permanently!

Get Help for a Field—Q&A allows you to Define Custom Help for any field. If the current field has Custom Help defined for it then you can press F1 to display that help screen. If the field does not have a custom help screen you will see Q&A standard help screen about Add Data. Also, pressing F1 from the Custom Help screen will display the Q&A help screen.

Navigate Around a Record—You may move through the record with a number of different keystrokes. Alternatively, the form may be programmed to control movements of the cursor. If there is no programming involved, the following keys will act as described:

Arrows—The up and down arrow keys will move the cursor to the field directly above or below the current field. In a multiline field, they will move the cursor one line up or down. The left and right arrow keys will move the cursor one character to the left or right.

End—Pressing the End key once will move the cursor to the end of the current field, or the current line of a multiline field. Pressing End a second time will move the cursor to the beginning of the last field on the current page of the form. Pressing End a third time will put the cursor at the beginning of the last field on the last page of this form.

Enter—The Enter key will move the cursor to the next field. If the current field is a multiline field then the cursor will go to the beginning of the next line of this field.

Home—Pressing the Home key once will move the cursor to the beginning of the current field, or the current line of a multiline field. Pressing Home a second time will move the cursor to the beginning of the first field on the current page of the form. Pressing Home a third time will put the cursor at the beginning of the first field on the first page of this form.

PgUp and PgDn—PgUp will move the cursor to the first field on the previous page. Likewise, PgDn will move the cursor to the first field on the next page. If there is no previous or next page, the cursor will stay in the current field.

Tab—Tab will always move the cursor to the next field whether the current field is multiline or not. Likewise, Shift-Tab will move the cursor to the previous field.

Print a Record—At any time you may print the current record by pressing F2. This will display the Print Options screen. Optionally, you can press F8 and change the Define Page. When finished, press F10 to print the form according to your specifications. The form will appear on paper as it appears on screen.

Save a Record—Press F10 to save the current record and move on to the next. Press Shift-F10 to save the current record and exit the database. Press F9 to save the current record and backup to the previous record.

Set Calculation Options—If necessary, you may change some options concerning the execution of a file's programming statements. To do this, press Shift-F8 at any time to view or change the following options:

Calculation Mode—In Automatic Mode, all calculation statements are executed automatically whenever any field's value is changed. In Manual Mode, calc statements are executed only when the user presses F8. In either mode, programming that is On Field Entry (OFE) or On Field Exit (OFX) will not be executed.

Main Program before Field Exit?—This option controls the situation when a field contains OFX programming and the Calculation Mode is Automatic. Whenever that field's value is changed, Q&A needs to know which programming to execute first because the results of one calculation may affect the other. YES will execute the Calc statements before the OFX statements, while NO will execute the OFX first. This option is not used if Calculation Mode is set to Manual.

View a Field's Restrictions—You may view the restrict values of any field by pressing Alt-F7 while in that field. Q&A will normally display the restriction in a box below the field, but if the restrict values for the field contain only a list of valid selections for the field, then Alt-F7 will display an alphabetized pick list of the selections. To select something from this list, first highlight it, then press Enter. You may highlight an option by typing the first few letters of the choice until it is highlighted.

Valid Keystrokes:

Ctrl-F2—Print the current record and all the selected records after it

F2—Print record

F3—Delete record

Alt-F4—Ignore template

Alt-F5—Auto-type the current time

Ctrl-F5—Auto-type the current date

Shift-F5—Copy the entire previous record onto the current one

F5—Copy the current field from the previous record into the current field

F6—Expand the current field

Alt-F7—View restrictions

F7—Move directly to Search/Update mode

Ctrl-F8—Reset @Number (see *@Number* in the Programming Chapter)

Shift-F8—Set Calculation Options

F8—Calculate programming statements on this record

Shift-F9—Menu bypass to several Customize and Program Menu choices.

F9—Save record and move to previous record

Shift-F10—Save current record and exit

F10—Save current record and continue

Ctrl-Home—Move to the first record added

Ctrl-End—Move to the last record added

See Also: *Calculation Mode Programming* in the Programming Chapter.

Customize a File to change a field's format or default value.

Define Custom Help

Define Page in the General Chapter.

Design a New File to change the form layout, or add or delete fields.

Field Editor

Navigation Statements in the Programming Chapter to program the form to control cursor movements.

On Field Entry and Exit Programming in the Programming Chapter to create OFE and OFX programming statements.

Print Options in the General Chapter.

Remove to delete many records at once.

Restrict Values to add a list of valid options to any field.

Search/Update to modify records that were already added.

Assign Access Rights

Menu Path: File | Design File | Secure a File | Assign Access Rights

Description: Assigns User IDs and Passwords to individual users of the database. Also controls the functions each user can perform on the database.

Procedure:
1. Select Assign Access Rights from the Security Menu.

2. On the List of Users/Groups enter the User ID (up to 20 characters) of the user you want to create, or alternatively, if you are editing a User ID, select it from the list.

3. On the Access Control screen set the following options:

   Initial Password—The Password that allows the user to gain access to the file; it can be up to 20 characters long.

   Can Assign Password Rights—Should this user have the ability to set and change Access rights to this database? At least one user must have this right. This right is an Administrative right.

   Can Change Design and Program—Should this user be allowed to change the form design and the form programming? This right is an Administrative right.

   Can Mass Delete—Can this user remove records using the Remove option from the File Menu?

   Can Delete Individual Records—Can this user use the F3 key to delete records during data entry?

   Can Run Mass Update—Should this user be allowed to perform Mass Update operations on this database?

   Can Design/Redesign Reports—Should this user be able to design new reports and redesign old reports for this database? All users can print reports.

   Can Enter/Edit Data—Should this user have read/write or read-only access to the database? YES indicates read/write access and NO indicates read-only access.

4. Press F10 to save the Access Control screen.

5. Q&A will ask if you want to edit another User ID. If you select YES, you should repeat steps 2 through 5. NO will take you back to the Security Menu.

Notes: Users who have neither of the two Administrative rights can be placed into Field Restriction groups. These groups allow access to be controlled at the field level.

Q&A will not allow you to leave Assign Access Rights without at least one user having Assign Password rights.

The first time a password protected file is accessed during each session, Q&A will display the User ID and Password Entry Box. Subsequently, when the file is accessed Q&A will not prompt for the user ID and Password.

See Also: *Field Level Security* to control which fields users can access.

User ID and Password Box in the General Chapter for details on entering Passwords.

Backup Database

Menu Path: File I Utilities I Backup Database

Description: Makes a backup copy of a database.

Procedure: 1. Select Backup Database from the Utilities Menu.

2. Type the name of the database to backup and press Enter.

3. Type the name of the backup copy of the database and press Enter.

Notes: This command makes a copy of the database. If the database is too big to fit on the disk (i.e., a floppy diskette), Q&A will display an "Out of Disk Space" message. You will not be prompted for additional disks, and the backup will not be made.

Change Define Page Defaults

Menu Path: File I Print I Set Global Options I Change Define Page Defaults

Description: Changes the default Define Page options in effect during Design/Redesign a Spec. The Define Page options displayed when printing a single record (i.e., during Add Data or Search/Update by pressing F2) can be changed via the Change Single Form Page Default option.

Procedure: 1. Select Change Define Page Defaults or Change
Single Form Page Default from the Global Op-
tions Menu.

2. Define the page to your preference.

3. Press F10 to save the new defaults.

See Also: *Define Page* in the General Chapter for information
on the available Define Page options.

Change Print Options Defaults to set the Print Options for new Print Specs or single record printing
from Add Data or Search/Update.

Change Palette

Menu Path: File I Design File I Customize a File I Change Palette

Description: Allows selection of color, highlighting, and underlining for the database display.

Procedure: 1. Select Change Palette from the Customize Menu.

2. Press F6 and F8 to select one of the seven available palette choices.

3. Press F10 when the desired palette is on screen.

Notes: You may type text on this screen to see how text will
be displayed in the fields for each palette choice.

**Valid
Keystrokes:**   Ctrl-F6—Move directly to Add Data

F6—Display the previous palette

F7—Move directly to Search/Update

F8—Display the next palette

Change Print Options Defaults

Menu Path: File I Print I Set Global Options I Change Print Options Defaults

Description: Changes the default Print Options in effect during
Design/Redesign a Spec. The Print Options displayed
when printing a single record (i.e., during Add Data
or Search/Update by pressing F2) can be changed via
the Change Single Form Print Defaults option.

Procedure: 1. Select Change Print Options Defaults or Change Single Form Print Defaults from the Global Options Menu.

2. Modify the Print Options to your preference.

3. Press F10 to save the new options.

See Also: *Print Options* in the General Chapter for information on the available Print Options.

Change Define Page Defaults to set the default Define Page options for new Print Specs or single record printing from Add Data or Search/Update.

_____ *Change Single Form Page Defaults*

See *Change Define Page Defaults*

_____ *Change Single Form Print Defaults*

See *Change Print Options Defaults*

_____ *Coordinate Printing*

See *Design/Redesign a Spec*

_____ *Copy*

Menu Path: File | Copy

Description: Allows the database design to be copied without its records. Also allows the records to be copied without the form design.

Procedure: 1. Select Copy from the File Menu.

2. Type the name of the file you want to copy and press Enter.

3. The Copy Menu displays the following options:

   Copy Design Only—Copies the form design of the database to a new file. This copies all reports, Print Specs, saved specs, and programming to the new file. The records are not copied, nor are the Intelligent Assistant and Query Guide information copied.

Copy Design with IA/QG—Copies the form design of the database to a new file. This copies all reports, Print Specs, saved specs, and programming to the new file. The records are not copied, but the Intelligent Assistant and Query Guide information are copied.

Copy Selected Records—Copies selected records from the current database to another one.

See Also: *Copy Design*

Copy Selected Records

Copy a Print Spec _____

See *Rename/Delete/Copy a Spec*

Copy Design _____

Menu Path: File I Copy I Copy Design Only

File I Copy I Copy Design with IA/QG

Description: Copies the form design of the current database to a new file. This copies all reports, Print Specs, saved specs, and programming to the new file, but the records are not copied. The Intelligent Assistant and Query Guide information are only copied when you select the Copy Design with IA/QG option.

Procedure: 1. Select Copy from the File Menu.

2. Type the name of the file to copy and press Enter.

3. Select Copy Design Only or Copy Design with IA/QG from the Copy Menu.

4. Type the name of the destination file and press Enter.

See Also: *Copy Selected Records*

Copy Selected Records _____

Menu Path: File I Copy I Copy Selected Records

Description: Allows selected records to be copied from the current database to another database.

Procedure:
1. Select Copy from the File Menu.
2. Type the name of the file to copy and press Enter.
3. Select Copy Selected Records from the Copy Menu.
4. Type the name of the destination file and press Enter.
5. On the Retrieve Spec enter values to choose which records you want copied. Optionally, press F8 to sort the selected records, then press F10.
6. On the Merge Spec enter values to indicate the order in which the fields should be copied to the destination database.
7. Press F10 to begin the copy.

Notes: Esc during the copy procedure will cancel the process but all records copied up to that point will remain in the destination file.

See Also: *Retrieve Spec*

Sort Spec

Merge Spec

Copy Design

Export Data to move records from a Q&A database to another type of file.

Create Application Menu

Menu Path: File | Design File | Customize Application | Create Application Menu

Description: Creates and edits custom menus. This is an alternative to the Create Menu option on the Macro Menu.

See Also: *Create Menu* in the Macros and Menus Chapter for details on creating custom menus.

Customize a File

Menu Path: File | Design File | Customize a File

Description: Displays the Customize Menu. The Customize Menu allows adjustment of field level details for a database. These adjustments can include setting default values or creating custom help screens for a field.

Procedure: 1. Select Customize a File from the Design Menu.

2. Enter the name of the file to customize.

3. The Customize Menu provides the following options:

Format Values—Identifies what type of information will be in each field and how that information will be formatted.

Restrict Values—Restricts data entry into fields by requiring that specific criteria be met.

Field Template—Aids data entry by controlling the format of text fields with standard formats (i.e., phone numbers).

Set Initial Values—Creates default entries for a field.

Speed up Searches—Indexes commonly searched fields, resulting in increased retrieval speed of records.

Define custom help—Creates a user-definable help screen for each field.

Change palette—Selects the color, shading, and underlining to be used in displaying the database.

See Also: *Format Values*
Restrict Values
Field Template
Set Initial Values
Speed Up Searches
Define Custom Help
Change Palette

Customize Application

Menu Path: File I Design File I Customize Application

Description: Displays the Customize Application Menu. The Customize Application Menu allows the locking of data
files and macro files and the creation of Custom
Menus.

Procedure: 1. Select Customize Application from the Design
Menu.

2. The Customize Application Menu displays the following choices:

   Create Application Menu—This is an alternative
   way to create custom menus. Custom menus
   are also created through the Macro Menu.

   Lock Database—Locks desired areas of the database to keep all users from modifying those
   areas.

   Protect Macro File—Encrypts a macro file so it
   can no longer be edited.

See Also: *Create Menu* in the Macros and Menus Chapter to
create and use custom menus.

Lock Database

Protect Macro File in the Macros and Menus
Chapter

Declare Sharing Mode

Menu Path: File | Design File | Secure a File | Declare Sharing Mode

Description: Sets the file sharing mode Q&A will use in accessing
the database on networks.

Procedure: 1. Select Declare Sharing Mode from the Security
Menu.

2. Use the arrow keys to select one of the following:

   Automatic—Q&A determines what type of drive
   the database is stored on. If the database is on
   a dedicated network file server, Q&A will allow
   multiple users to share the database. If it is on
   a non-dedicated network file server, a distributed server network, or a local drive, concurrent sharing of the file by multiple users will be
   disallowed. This is the default setting.

Disallow—Disallows multiple users concurrent access to the database.

Allow—Always allows multiple users concurrent access to the database. To use this setting with files on a local hard drive, the DOS SHARE command must be loaded in your AUTO-EXEC.BAT file.

3. Press F10 to save the selection.

Notes: The Allow setting should be used when files are located in non-dedicated network environments, distributed networks, or multitasking environments.

Define Custom Help _____

Menu Path: File I Define File I Customize a File I Define Custom Help

Description: Creates a custom help screen for selected fields. This help screen can be accessed during Add Data and Search/Update by moving to the field and pressing F1.

Procedure: 1. Select Define Custom Help from the Customize Menu.

2. Press F6 and F8 to move to the desired field.

3. Type the text of your help screen for the highlighted field.

4. Repeat steps 2 and 3 until finished.

5. Press F5 and select the appropriate Help Mode:

Concurrent—In this mode, the custom help screen remains visible at the same time that the user is editing the field. After pressing F1 once to display the first custom help screen, any time the user edits a field that also has a custom help screen it is displayed automatically.

Nonconcurrent—In this mode, the user cannot edit a field while its custom help screen is displayed. The user must first press any key to clear the help screen in order to edit the field.

Cancel—Clears the Help Mode box without changing the selected Help Mode.

**Valid
Keystrokes:**   F5—Select the Help Mode

Ctrl-F6—Move directly to Add Data

F6—Move the highlighted bar to the previous field

F7—Move directly to Search/Update

F8—Move the highlighted bar to the next field

See Also: *@Help* in the Programming Chapter to display custom help screens automatically.

_____ *Define Page, File*

See *Define Page* in the General Chapter.

_____ *Delete a Print Spec*

See *Rename/Delete/Copy a Spec*

_____ *Design a New File*

Menu Path: File I Design File I Design a New File

Description: Facilitates creation of a new database including the visual representation (form design), and assignment of field types.

Procedure: 1. Select Design a New File from the Design Menu.

2. Type the name to give the new database, and press Enter. All Q&A databases must have a .DTF extension, and it will be appended to the name entered.

3. At the blank screen that appears, lay out the form as you would like it to appear when entering data. Follow these steps to add fields to the form layout:

a. Use the cursor-moving keys to position the cursor wherever you would like to place a field label. Type the field label (usually a descriptive name of the field contents), followed by a colon (:) or a less than symbol (<). If you use the colon to signify the beginning of the field, the colon will be visible whenever the form is encountered. On the other hand, the less than symbol will be hidden during any access to the form. Field labels are optional, however, Q&A does provide an "internal" field label for use in referencing the field in programming, or reports. This internal field label can be modified by the user through the Set Field Names command.

b. Optionally, you may position the cursor where you would like the field to end, and type a greater than symbol (>). A field ends if it encounters the right side of the screen, the start of another field, background characters, the greater than symbol, or the end of the page.

c. Repeat steps a and b until all the fields have been laid out on the form.

4. Press F10 when the form has been laid out.

5. After the form and database design have been saved, the Format Spec will appear. All fields default to type Text, so they will all have T's in them.

6. Assign the desired field types, using the available codes shown in Table 2.1:

Table 2.1.   Design Format Codes

Code	Type	Usage
T	Text	To enter any characters—alphabetic, numeric, and punctuation.
N	Number	To enter only numeric characters. Allows arithmetic calculations and numeric sorting.
M	Money	To enter numeric values that represent monetary amounts.
K	Keyword	To enter multiple entries into single fields separated by semicolons for special retrieval.
D	Date	To enter date values.
H	Hours	To enter time values.
Y	Yes/No	To enter one of two possible conditions (i.e., Yes/ No, True/False).

To modify the Format code, move the cursor to the field for modification, and type in the new code. These formatting codes can also be modified at a later time through Format Values.

7. Press F10 upon completion of the Format Spec.

8. If you have money, number, date, or time fields on the form layout, the Global Format Options screen will apear. Change these options if required, and press F10.

Notes: The editor used for the form layout is a limited version of the Q&A word processor, so many operations will be identical in both. See the appropriate commands in the Write Chapter for additional information.

Table 2.2 represents the limits of a Q&A database:

Table 2.2. Database Limits

Item	Maximum Limit
Pages per record	10
Fields per record	2045
Fields per page	248
Characters per record	64,512
Characters per field	32,767
Records per database	16,000,000
Database Size	1024 Megabytes

Background Characters—Background text (appears on screen as a part of every form) can be placed on the form as long as it does not interfere with space defined for fields. To place background text or characters on the form (i.e., instructions, reminders, form headings, etc.) type in the text at the location you would like it to appear.

Multiple Line Fields—Fields are not restricted to a single line. Multiline fields are much the same as regular fields. They begin with either a colon (:) or a less than symbol (<); however a multiline field must end with a greater than symbol (>). If the start of the field is signified by a colon, then subsequent lines will begin at the left edge of the screen. If the start is signified by a less than symbol, then subsequent lines will be aligned with the less than symbol.

A multiline field cannot have any characters between the start and the end of the field. If you look at the space between the beginning of the field and the end of the field from left to right and then down to the next line, and you see any characters, then the fields will not appear as desired. In most cases the field will be shorter than you expected. Multiline fields cannot have any background characters, or have fields on either side of them except on the right side of the last line.

Drawing Boxes—Boxes can be drawn on the form to separate different areas of the form, or call attention to specific areas of the form. To draw boxes place the cursor where you would like to begin the line or box, and follow these steps:

a. Press F8 to display the Options Menu.

b. Select Lay Out Page, and then press the Enter key to move the cursor into the submenu.

c. Select Draw from the submenu.

d. Draw the line or box you wish using the arrow keys on the numeric keypad. To draw double lines, hold down the shift key and then use the arrow keys. To lift the drawing pen, press F6. This will allow you to move the pen to a different location using the arrow keys without actually drawing a line. To begin drawing again, press F6. To erase a line, press F8. Now as you move the cursor using the arrow keys, the character under the cursor will be erased. To begin drawing again, press F8.

e. When you have finished drawing, press F10 to return to editing the form.

Other options are available when laying out the form. These options are a subset of the options available when editing a document in Write. Those features not available from the Options Menu are disabled. Table 2.3 is a list of available options from the Options Menu that appears by pressing F8:

Table 2.3.   Design Options

Option	Description
Lay Out Page	
Set Tabs	Sets preset positions on each horizontal line that can be jumped to directly by pressing the tab key.
Draw	Draws lines and boxes.
Document	
Insert	Inserts a document in the form layout at the cursor position.
Align Text	
Left	Aligns text based with the left side of the form.
Center	Centers text on the form.
Block Operation	
Copy	Makes a duplicate copy of the selected text.
Move	Moves selected text to a new place on the form.
Delete	Deletes selected text from the form.
Copy to File	Makes a duplicate copy of the selected text; places it in a separate file.
Move to File	Moves selected text to separate file.
Print	Prints selected text.
Capitalize	Makes all characters in the selected text uppercase.
Lowercase	Makes all characters in the selected text lowercase.
Title	Uppercases the first character of all words that usually appear uppercased in titles.
Other Options	
Spellcheck	Checks spelling of the form layout.
Spellcheck Word	Checks spelling of a single word.
Thesaurus	Displays synonyms for the word the cursor is on.
Statistics	Displays the number of words, lines, and paragraphs on the form.
Search and Replace	Searches for, and optionally replaces words or phrases.
Restore	Restores text that was most recently deleted.
Go to Page/Line	Places cursor on the specified line of the specified page.
Calculate	Adds, subtracts, multiplies, and divides numbers on the form layout.

Valid Keystrokes:	Shift-F1—Checks spelling of the form
	Ctrl-F1—Checks spelling of a word
	Alt-F1—Checks thesaurus for a word
	Ctrl-F2—Prints text block
	F3—Delete text block
	Ctrl-F3—Counts words, lines, and paragraphs
	Shift-F5—Moves text block to file
	Alt-F5—Moves text block
	F5—Copies text block to file
	Ctrl-F5—Copies text block
	F7—Search and Replace
	Shift-F7—Restores most recently deleted text
	F8—Displays Options Menu
	Alt-F9—Performs row/column calculations
See Also:	*Format Values* for information on the different field types.
	Write Chapter for information on the commands on the Options Menu.
	Set Field Names for information on setting the internal field names.

Design File _____

Menu Path:	File | Design File
Description:	Displays the Design Menu. The Design Menu accesses commands used in creating, modifying, customizing, programming, and securing a Q&A database.
Procedure:	1. Select Design from the File Menu.
	2. The Design Menu has the following options:

> **Design a New File**—Creates a new database.
>
> **Redesign a File**—Modifies an existing database.
>
> **Customize a File**—Modifies customizable aspects of a database such as field types, custom help,

database palettes, restriction values, initial values, speed-up searches, and field templates.

Program a File—Accesses commands to aid programming, and to implement programming such as the lookup table, setting field names, setting read only fields, form navigation, and actual programming of the form.

Secure a File—Sets different levels of restriction on access to a database or fields in a database by multiple users, defines the sharing mode to access a database, and specifies the User ID and Password to use for the Xlookup programming statement.

Customize Application—Allows definition of custom menus, locking of a database, or protection of a macro file.

See Also: *Design a New File*
Redesign a File
Program a File
Secure a File
Customize Application

Design/Redesign a Spec

Menu Path: File | Print | Design/Redesign a Spec

Description: Creates and saves a collection of specs (Print Specs) that can be used to print selected record in a specified fashion. Allows the modification of existing Print Specs.

Procedure: 1. Select Design/Redesign a Spec from the Print Menu.

2. Choose or type the name of the Print Spec that you would like design or redesign, and press F10.

3. At the Retrieve Spec, enter the restriction to use in selecting the records to print. You may optionally press F8 to access the Sort Spec. Press F10 upon completion of the Retrieve and Sort Specs.

4. At the Fields Spec, enter the appropriate codes controlling which fields print, and their location

on the printed page. You may press F6 to expand the field if the codes will not fit in the space displayed on the screen. Optionally, you may leave the Fields Spec blank. Doing so will print the form as it appears on the screen (including all fields, boxes drawn, etc.). The following are the two different styles of printing available:

Free-Form Style—Used for simple placement of fields on the printed page. The primary codes are as follows:

   X—prints the field, and moves to the next line before printing subsequent fields. To skip multiple lines, add a comma, and a number representing the number of lines to move down.

   +—prints the field, and skips a single space before printing subsequent fields. To skip multiple spaces, add a comma, and a number representing the number of spaces to skip.

To specify the order in which to print the fields, precede the codes with a number specifying the order. Omitting this number will result in the fields printing in the on-screen order, from top-left to bottom-right.

The following code may be used with either of the two previously mentioned codes:

   E—prints the entire field contents, even if all the data is not visible on screen.

Coordinate Style—Used for specific placement of fields on the printed page. Specify the location on the printed page to print the field contents by entering the line number from the top of the page and the character position from the left edge of the page (i.e., 6,24 will print that field on the sixth line down, 24 characters from the left edge of the page). Optionally, the row and column coordinates can be specified in centimeters or inches. To specify the coordinates in centimeters type a cm after the numbers; for inches type a quote ('') symbol after the numbers.

5. Press F10 upon completion of the Fields Spec.

6. Set the options on the Print Options screen, and optionally set the options on the Define Page screen by pressing F8. Save the Print Spec upon completion of the Print Options by pressing F10.

7. You will have the option to print records according to the newly designed Print Spec. Answer YES to print the records, or NO to return to the Print Menu.

Notes: To print the label of the field, regardless of the Print Field Labels setting on the Print Options screen, enter an L into the field on the Fields Spec. To change the label that Q&A will print, enter the text of the new label in parentheses following the L.

You may specify how much of each field prints by entering an additional number on the Fields Spec representing the maximum number of characters to print.

A field can be enhanced or fonted by pressing Shift-F6 when the cursor is in the field at the Fields Spec. Once an enhancement has been chosen, highlight the code in the field, and press F10. To enhance the field label, highlight the L code.

Valid Keystrokes: F6—Expand Field on the Fields Spec

Shift-F6—Text Enhancements and Fonts Menu on the Fields Spec

F9—Go back to the Retrieve Spec from the Fields Spec

See Also: *Retrieve Spec* for information on retrieving records for Print Specs.

Sort Spec for information on sorting records for Print Specs.

Print Options in the General Chapter.

Define Page in the General Chapter.

Edit Lookup Table

Menu Path: File I Design File I Program a File I Edit Lookup Table

Description:	Adds to or modifies the columns of the built-in lookup table in a Q&A database. This information can be accessed through programming statements.
Procedure:	1. Select Edit Lookup Table from the Program Menu.
	2. Type values into the Key column, and the four additional data columns. The Key column is used like an index to access data in the other four columns. It should contain a unique value (i.e., part numbers in an inventory database).
	Information entered into the four data columns is associated with the entry in the Key column on the same line (i.e., price and description of a part in an inventory database). Data corresponding to a particular type of key value should be kept in the same data column (i.e., prices in column 1, and descriptions in column 2 for all part numbers).
	There is only one Lookup Table in a database, therefore items in the Lookup Table do not have to be related. You can enter 10 lines of part numbers and associated data, and then enter 10 lines of state abbreviations and associated data, and access both sets of information by supplying the correct key value in the programming statement.
	3. Press F10 when you have finished editing.
Notes:	The lookup table can hold up to 64,000 characters of data. Information can be accessed through the Lookup, @Lookup, Lookupr, or @Lookupr programming statements.
	To insert a row, place the cursor in the first character position in the Key column, make sure you are in Insert mode, and press Enter.
Valid Keystrokes:	Tab—To move the cursor one column to the right
	Shift-Tab—To move the cursor one column to the left
	Pgup—To move the cursor up a page
	Pgdn—To move the cursor down a page
	Shift-F4—To delete a row
	F6—To expand the space so additional data can be added

See Also: *Lookup Functions and Statements* in the Programming Chapter for information on how to access data from the Lookup Table.

_____ *Export Data*

Menu Path: File | Utilities | Export Data

Description: Exports data from a Q&A database to variety of data formats.

Procedure: 1. Select Export data from the Utilities Menu.

2. Select the format of the output file. The following are the available formats:

DIF

Fixed ASCII

Standard ASCII

dBase II/III/IV

Paradox 2.0/3.x

See Also: *Import Data*

Export to DIF

Export to Standard ASCII

Export to Fixed ASCII

Export to dBase II/III/IV

Export to Paradox 2.0/3.x

_____ *Export to dBase II/III/IV*

Menu Path: File | Utilities | Export Data | dBase II/dBase III/ dBase IV

Description: Exports data from an existing Q&A database to a newly created dBase II/III/IV file.

Procedure: 1. Select dBase II, dBase III, or dBase IV from the Export Menu.

2. Type the path and name of the Q&A database from which the data is to be exported, and press Enter.

3. Type the name for the newly created dBase file (including the .DBF extension), and press Enter.

4. At the Retrieve Spec, enter the retrieve criteria for the records to export. Optionally, to sort the exported data, press F8 to access the Sort Spec. Press F10 upon completion of the Retrieve and Sort Specs.

5. At the Merge Spec, enter a numeric value into the fields to export. Upon completion of the Merge Spec, press F10.

See Also: *Import from dBase II/III/IV*

Retrieve Spec

Sort Spec

Merge Spec

Export to DIF _____

Menu Path: File I Utilities I Export Data I DIF

Description: Exports data from an existing Q&A database to a newly created DIF (Data Interchange Format) file. The DIF file format is made up of "vectors" and "tuples." A DIF vector corresponds to a field, and a DIF tuple corresponds to a record.

Procedure: 1. Select DIF from the Export Menu.

2. Type the name of the Q&A database from which the data is to be exported, and press Enter.

3. Type the name for the newly created DIF file and press Enter.

4. At the Retrieve Spec, enter the retrieve criteria for the records to export. Optionally, to sort the exported data, press F8 to access the Sort Spec. Press F10 upon completion of the Retrieve and Sort Specs.

5. At the Merge Spec, enter a numeric value into those fields to export. Upon completion of the Merge Spec, press F10.

See Also: *Import from DIF*
                     Retrieve Spec
                     Sort Spec
                     Merge Spec

_____ *Export to Fixed ASCII*

Menu Path: File | Utilities | Export Data | Fixed ASCII

Description: Exports data from an existing Q&A database to a
                  newly created Fixed ASCII file. The Fixed ASCII file
                  format separates each record onto its own line (de-
                  limited by carriage return and linefeed), and the
                  same fields on different records begin at the same
                  character column.

Procedure: 1. Select Fixed ASCII from the Export Menu.

                  2. Type the name of the Q&A database from which
                     the data is to be exported, and press Enter.

                  3. Type the name for the newly created Fixed ASCII
                     file, and press Enter.

                  4. At the Retrieve Spec, enter the retrieve criteria for
                     the records to export. Optionally, to sort the ex-
                     ported data, press F8 to access the Sort Spec.
                     Press F10 upon completion of the Retrieve and
                     Sort Specs.

                  5. At the Merge Spec, type two numbers into each
                     field from which data is to be exported. The first
                     number is the column number in the Fixed ASCII
                     file where the field value to be exported will be-
                     gin. The second number is the maximum length of
                     the field value. Press F10 upon completion of the
                     Merge Spec.

See Also: *Import from Fixed ASCII*
                  Export to Standard ASCII
                  Retrieve Spec
                  Sort Spec

Export to Paradox 2.0/3.x _____

Menu Path: File I Utilities I Export Data I Paradox 2.0/3.x

Description: Exports data from an existing Q&A database to a newly created Paradox 2.0/3.x file.

Procedure:
1. Select Paradox 2.0/3.x from the Export Menu.
2. Type the name of the Q&A database from which the data is to be exported, and press Enter.
3. Type the name for the newly created Paradox 2.0/3.x file, and press Enter.
4. At the Retrieve Spec, enter the retrieve criteria for the records to export. Optionally, to sort the exported data, press F8 to access the Sort Spec. Press F10 upon completion of the Retrieve and Sort Specs.
5. At the Merge Spec, enter a numeric value into those fields to export. Upon completion of the Merge Spec, press F10.

See Also: *Import from Paradox 2.0/3.x*
Retrieve Spec
Sort Spec
Merge Spec

Export to Standard ASCII _____

Menu Path: File I Utilities I Export Data I Standard ASCII

Description: Exports data from a Q&A database to a newly created Standard ASCII file. The Standard ASCII file format separates each record onto its own line (delimited by carriage return and linefeed), and separates each field from the next by a comma.

Procedure:
1. Select Standard ASCII from the Export Menu.
2. Type the name of the Q&A database from which the data is to be exported, and press Enter.
3. Type the name for the newly created Standard ASCII file, and press Enter.
4. At the Retrieve Spec, enter the retrieve criteria for the records to export. Optionally, to sort the ex-

ported data, press F8 to access the Sort Spec.
Press F10 upon completion of the Retrieve and
Sort Specs.

5. At the Merge Spec, enter a numeric value into the
fields to export. Upon completion of the Merge
Spec, press F10.

6. At the ASCII Options screen, set the following options for the exported file:

Quotes Around Text—Selecting YES will put
quotes around fields of type Text, and selecting
NO will export Text data with no quotes. The
default value is YES.

Field Delimiter—Specify the character used to
separate one field from the next. The options
are Return, Semicolon, Comma, and Space.
Comma is the default.

Export Field Template—Selecting YES will export
data with field templates, and selecting NO will
export only the data omitting any field templates. The default value is NO.

7. Press F10 upon completing the ASCII Options.

See Also: *Export to Fixed ASCII* for information on another
ASCII format that can be created.

Import from Standard ASCII

Retrieve Spec

Sort Spec

Merge Spec

Field Template for information on how to set field
templates.

_____ *Field Editor*

Description: Allows manually entered data in a field to be greater
than the size available on the screen.

Procedure: 1. Press F6 in a field where you would like to enter
information that will not fit in the area on the
screen. Q&A will display an eight-line area on the
screen for entering information.

2. Enter the information into the Field Editor. All basic editing and cursor movement keys are available (i.e., arrow keys for cursor movement, Enter to move to the beginning of the next line, Backspace to delete the previous character, etc.). Press F10 when you are done to close the Field Editor.

Notes: The Field Editor is available in both Add Data and Search/Update, but only in Text or Keyword fields. It can also be used in the Program Spec and the Restrict Values Spec to enter long values into any field. It is a limited version of the word processor, and can hold up to 32,000 characters.

Operations that automatically enter data into fields (i.e., Posting, Importing, Mass Updating, etc.) are not limited by the space on the screen. Any data values placed automatically in fields where the screen area is not large enough can be edited using the Field Editor.

Those options not available in the Field Editor are disabled. For detailed information on any options or commands, see the appropriate command in the Write Chapter. Pressing F8 displays the Options Menu shown in Table 2.4:

Table 2.4. Field Editor Options

Option	Description
Lay Out Page	
Draw	Draws lines and boxes.
Document	
Insert	Inserts a document in the field at the cursor position.
Block Operation	
Copy	Makes a duplicate copy of the selected text.
Move	Moves selected text to a new place in the field.
Delete	Deletes selected text from the field.
Copy to File	Makes a duplicate copy of the selected text; places it in a separate file.
Move to File	Moves selected text to separate file.
Print	Prints selected text.
Capitalize	Makes all characters in the selected text uppercase.

(continued)

Table 2.4. Field Editor Options *(continued)*

Option	Description
Lowercase	Makes all characters in the selected text lowercase.
Title	Uppercases the first character of all words that usually appear uppercased in titles.
Other Options	
Spellcheck	Checks spelling of the field contents.
Spellcheck Word	Checks spelling of a single word.
Thesaurus	Displays synonyms for the word at the cursor.
Statistics	Displays the number of words, lines, and paragraphs in the field.
Search and Replace	Searches for, and optionally replaces, words or phrases.
Restore	Restores text that was most recently deleted.
Go to Page/Line	Places cursor on the specified line.
Calculate	Adds, subtracts, multiplies, and divides numbers in the field.

Valid Keystrokes:

Shift-F1—Checks spelling of the field

Ctrl-F1—Checks spelling of a word

Alt-F1—Checks thesaurus for a word

Ctrl-F2—Prints text block

F3—Delete text block

Ctrl-F3—Counts words, lines, and paragraphs

Shift-F5—Moves text block to file

Alt-F5—Moves text block

Ctrl-F5—Copies text block to file

F5—Copies text block

F7—Search and Replace

Shift-F7—Restores most recently deleted text

F8—Displays options menu

Alt-F9—Performs row/column calculations

See Also:

Add Data

Program Form

Restrict Values

Search/Update

Write Chapter for additional information on basic
editing or those options available.

Field Level Security

Menu Path: File I Design File I Secure a File I Field Level Security

Description: Allows up to eight users or groups of users to each
have a different view of the database. These views
are created by hiding fields and making others read-
only.

Procedure:
1. Assign User IDs and Passwords to all users of the
   database. See the *Assign Access Rights* command.

2. Select Field Level Security from the Security
   Menu.

3. On the List of Field Security Specs enter the name
   of the Security Spec (up to 31 characters) you
   want to create, or alternatively, if you are editing
   a Security Spec, select it from the list. A total of
   eight different restriction groups can be created for
   each database.

4. On the Field Security Spec, type one of the following into each field:

   W—Read and Write Access—Users can see and
   edit values in this field.

   R—Read-Only Access—Users can see information
   in this field, but they cannot edit it.

   N—No Access—Users cannot see this field on the
   screen. They cannot see its contents or its field
   label.

5. Press F10 to save the Field Security Spec.

6. On the User Selection screen, you can enter the
   User IDs of users to include in this restriction
   group. Press Alt-F7 for a list of available users.
   The list of available users will include all User IDs
   for this database except users that have either Assign Password or Change Design and Program access rights. Also excluded are all users already assigned to a group. If there are no available users,
   you will get a message to that effect. A maximum

of 120 users can be assigned to any one restriction group.

7. Press F10 to save the User Selection screen.

Notes: All On Field Entry and On Field Exit programming in fields that are hidden or read-only will be executed when a user moves "over" those fields.

Users in field restriction groups with one or more fields marked as N for No Access will not be able to see Named Specs that include those hidden fields. All Named Specs that use fields that are hidden will not be visible on their lists.

See Also: *Assign Access Rights*

Using Named Specs in the General Chapter for information on using Named Specs.

Field Navigation

Menu Path: File | Design File | Program a File | Field Navigation

Description: Accepts statements that use Q&A's built-in navigation statements for controlling cursor movement when adding or updating data.

Procedure: 1. Select Field Navigation from the Program Menu.

2. Place the cursor in the field to enter a navigation statement.

3. Enter the navigation statement. If you cannot fit the statement in the space available on the screen, press F6 for additional space.

4. Repeat steps 2 and 3 until all necessary fields have navigation programming.

5. Press F10 to save the Navigation Spec.

See Also: *Navigation Statements* in the Programming Chapter for the available navigation statements.

Field Print Options

See *Print Options* in the General Chapter for descriptions of the available choices.

Field Template _____

Menu Path: File | Design File | Customize a File | Field Template

Description: Aids data entry by controlling the format of text fields with standard formats (i.e., phone numbers). The template supplies the user with a stencil of how the data should look and the user simply fills in the blanks.

Procedure: 1. Select Field Template from the Customize Menu.

2. Enter a template into the desired text fields. The cursor will skip over fields that are not text because templates can only be placed on text fields.

3. Press F10 when finished.

Notes: A field template consists of two parts, the template itself (i.e., the parenthesis and the dash for a phone number), and the data characters (i.e., the numbers of a phone number). Template characters can be any symbol, letter, or number; they form the stencil for the data. The data characters are represented in the template by the following symbols:

$—Any letter or number can be typed at this position.

@—Only letters A–Z and a–z can be typed at this position.

 # or 9—Only numbers 0–9 can be typed at this location.

If one of the data symbols ($,@,# or 9) is needed as a template character, precede it with a backslash character (\).

When retrieving data in a field with a template, do not include the template in the retrieval. To find the phone number (408) 123–4567, you should enter 4081234567 into that field on the Retrieve Spec. Also programming statements will treat template fields as if they have no template.

To enter a value in a template field that does not conform to the template, the user can press Alt-F4 to override the template for that one record.

Examples:	(###) ###-####	a phone number
	###-##-####	a Social Security number
	@@## ## @@	a part number like AX37 87 CD

| **Valid Keystrokes:** | Ctrl-F6—Move directly to Add Data |
| | F7—Move directly to Search/Update |

| **See Also:** | *Retrieve Spec* |

Format Values

| **Menu Path:** | File I Design File I Customize a File I Format Values |

Description: Identifies what type of information will be in each field and how that information will be formatted.

Procedure:
1. Select Format Values from the Customize Menu.

2. On the Format Spec enter a value in each field to indicate what type of information will be stored there. The default entry is T for Text (see Table 2.5 for a list of all codes).

Table 2.5. Format Codes

Code	Description
T	Text—Used for names, addresses, and comments.
N	Number—Used for quantities and scores.
M	Money—Holds prices, salaries, and sales figures.
K	Keyword—Used for lists of items separated by a semicolon (Hobbies: reading; chess). Every individual keyword can be searched for separately on the Retrieve Spec.
D	Date—Holds birthdays, and dates of sale. Automatically formats dates to display format.
H	Hours—Used for arrival times or the current time of day.
Y	Yes/No—Used for Yes/No, or True/False values.

Additionally, format options can be added in each field to control justification and other display options (see Table 2.6).

Table 2.6.   Format Options

Code	Meaning	Available Options
T	Text	JR—Justify Right
K	Keyword	JL—Justify Left
Y	Yes/No	JC—Justify Center
		U—All Uppercase
		L—All Lowercase
		I—Initial Caps
N	Number	JR, JL, JC—Justify Information
M	Money	C—Use commas for thousands (12,345)
		0–7—Number of decimal digits (for Number type only)
D	Date	JR, JL, JC—Justify Information
H	Hours	

3. Press F10 to continue. If you have selected any fields of types money (M), number (N), hours (H), or date (D), the Global Format Option Screen will be displayed.

4. Set each of the following options to the desired setting:

   Currency Symbol—The character typed here will appear with all money values in the database. The symbol can be any character.

   Currency Placement—Determines whether the currency symbol will appear before or after the money value.

   Space Between Symbol & Number—Indicates whether or not one space is desired between the currency symbol and the associated value.

   # of Currency Decimal Digits—Select from 0 through 7 decimal digits to display with every money value.

   Decimal Convention—Select the character to use as a decimal point. The American convention uses a period for a decimal point, and the European convention uses a comma for a decimal point.

   Time Display Format—Displays time in either a standard 12 hour am/pm mode, or in military

> or 24 hour mode. A third option uses military time with a period as a separator.
>
> **Date**—Select one of the 20 available options to control the display formats of all date fields from this database:

1—Mar 19, 1968	2—19 Mar 1968	3—3/19/68
4—19/3/68	5—3/19/1968	6—19/3/1968
7—03/19/68	8—19/03/68	9—03/19/1968
10—19/03/1968	11—March 19, 1968	12—19 March 1968
13—3-19-68	14—3-19-1968	15—03-19-68
16—03-19-1968	17—19.03.68	18—19.03.1968
19—1968-03-19	20—1968/03/19	

> 5. Press F10 when finished.

Notes: Initial caps fields will capitalize the first letter following a space or a period. This will be done as you leave the field.

Valid Keystrokes: F2—Print this spec

Ctrl-F6—Move directly to Add Data

F7—Move directly to Search/Update

F9—Go back to Format Spec

Free-Form Printing

See *Design/Redesign a Spec*

Import Data

Menu Path: File | Utilities | Import Data

Description: Imports data from various data formats into a Q&A database.

Procedure: 1. Select Import data from the Utilities Menu.

2. Select the format from which to import. The following are the available formats:

PFS or Professional File

IBM Filing Assistant

Lotus 123/Symphony

DIF

Fixed ASCII

Standard ASCII

dBase II/III/IV

Paradox 2.0/3.x

See Also: *Export Data*

Import from PFS/Pro File

Import from IBM Filing Assistant

Import from 123/Symphony

Import from DIF

Import from Fixed ASCII

Import from Standard ASCII

Import from dBase II/III/IV

Import from Paradox 2.0/3.x

Import from 123/Symphony _____

Menu Path: File I Utilities I Import Data I 123/Symphony

Description: Imports data from a Lotus 1-2-3 or Symphony spreadsheet into an existing Q&A database. Each spreadsheet row is treated as a record, and each spreadsheet cell is treated as a field.

Procedure: 1. Select 123/Symphony from the Import Menu.

2. Type the name of the spreadsheet to import and then press Enter.

3. Type the name of the Q&A database to receive the data and then press Enter.

4. At the Define Range screen select in one of the following manners the range of cells to import:

   To specify the cell coordinates of the range use the following options:

   From Column—The column of the top, leftmost cell to import.

   From Row—The row of the top, leftmost cell to import.

To Column—The column of the bottom, rightmost cell to import.

To Row—The row of the bottom, rightmost cell to import.

To specify a named range, type in the name of the range into the Range Name field. To see the named ranges in the spreadsheet, press the Pgup and Pgdn keys while in the Range Name field.

To import the entire spreadsheet, leave all entries blank.

5. Upon completing the Define Range screen, press F8 to display the Merge Spec, or press F10 to begin the import process.

6. If you chose to display the Merge Spec, enter the spreadsheet field numbers into the Q&A fields to receive data. The cell in the upper-left corner of the spreadsheet range corresponds to field 1, the cell directly to the right corresponds to field 2, and so on.

7. Press F10 upon completing the Merge Spec.

Notes: Spreadsheets created with Lotus 1-2-3 version 2.2 or earlier can be imported.

Lotus 1-2-3 version 2.2 spreadsheets may be password-protected, and cannot be imported unless the protection is removed.

For the import to succeed, spreadsheet cells must be saved as Values, and not as Formulas.

See Also: *Merge Spec*

Import from dBase II, III, IV

Menu Path: File I Utilities I Import Data I dBase II/III/IV

Description: Imports data from dBase II, III, or IV files into a new or existing Q&A database.

Procedure: 1. Select dBase II/III/IV from the Import Menu.

2. Type the name of the dBase file and press Enter.

3. Type the name of the Q&A database to receive the data and press Enter.

4. If the Q&A database does not exist, it will be created with a form design parallel to the file you are importing. The Format Spec will be displayed so that you can assign the correct information types to the fields in the new file. After completing the Format Spec, press F10. If the Format Spec contains number, money, date, or time fields, the Global Format Options screen will be displayed. After setting the Global Format Options to your preferences, press F10.

5. At the Merge Spec, enter the dBase field numbers into the Q&A fields to receive data. The first field in the dBase file structure is field 1, the second is field 2, and so on.

6. Press F10 upon completing the Merge Spec.

Notes: Up to 32K characters from each dBase memo field will be imported; however, a Q&A record has a limit of 64K characters per record. dBase numeric fields with more than 7 numbers to the right of the decimal point will be truncated.

See Also: *Merge Spec*

Format Values for information on the different format identifiers.

Export to dBase II/III/IV

Import from DIF

Menu Path: File I Utilities I Import data I DIF

Description: Imports a DIF (Data Interchange Format) file into an existing Q&A database. The DIF file format is made up of "vectors" and "tuples." A DIF vector corresponds to a field, and a DIF tuple corresponds to a record.

Procedure: 1. Select DIF from the Import Menu.

2. Type the name of the DIF file and press Enter.

3. Type the name of the Q&A database to receive the data and press Enter.

4. At the Merge Spec, enter the DIF field numbers into the Q&A fields to receive the data. The first

DIF vector corresponds to field 1, the second DIF vector corresponds to field 2, and so on.

5. Press F10 upon completing the Merge Spec.

See Also: *Merge Spec*

Export to DIF

Import from Fixed ASCII

Menu Path: File | Utilities | Import Data | Fixed ASCII

Description: Imports a Fixed ASCII file into an existing Q&A database. The Fixed ASCII file format separates each record onto its own line (delimited by carriage return and linefeed), and the same fields on different records begin at the same character column.

Procedure: 1. Select Fixed ASCII from the Import Menu.

2. Type the name of the Fixed ASCII file and press Enter.

3. Type the name of the Q&A database to receive the data and press Enter.

4. At the Merge Spec, type two numbers into each field to receive data. The first number is the column number in the Fixed ASCII file where the field value to be imported begins. The second number is the maximum length of the field value.

5. Press F10 upon completing the Merge Spec.

See Also: *Merge Spec*

Export to Fixed ASCII

Import from Standard ASCII

Import from IBM Filing Assistant

Menu Path: File | Utilities | Import Data | IBM Filing Asst

Description: Imports data from IBM Filing Assistant databases into a new or existing Q&A database.

Procedure: 1. Select IBM Filing Asst from the Import Menu.

2. Type the name of the IBM Filing Assistant database and press Enter.

3. Type the name of the Q&A database to receive the data and press Enter.

4. If the Q&A database does not exist, it will be created with a form design parallel to the file you are importing. The new form design will include any Retrieve Specs, Sort Specs, Print Specs, and Formulas contained in the IBM Filing Assistant file.

5. At the Format Spec, assign the correct information types to the fields in the new file. After completing the Format Spec, press F10. If the Format Spec contains number, money, date, or time fields, the Global Format Options screen will be displayed. After setting the Global Format Options to your preferences, press F10.

6. At the Merge Spec, enter the IBM Filing Assistant database field numbers into the Q&A fields to receive data. The first field on the top left of the IBM Filing Assistant form is field 1, the field to the right is field 2, and so on down the form.

7. Press F10 upon completing the Merge Spec.

Notes: If you are importing into an existing Q&A database, no Retrieve Specs, Sort Specs, Print Specs, or Formulas will be imported. In addition, the Format Spec, and the Global Format Options screen will not be displayed.

IBM Filing Assistant databases with attachment fields are handled differently. To import such a file, allow Q&A to create a new database for the destination. At the Format Spec, Escape from the import process, and redesign the database, adding the attachment fields after all other fields. Now restart the import process, using the original IBM Filing Assistant database as the source, and the newly redesigned database as the destination.

See Also: *Merge Spec*

Format Values for information on the different format identifiers.

Redesign a File for information on adding fields to a Q&A database.

_____ *Import from Paradox 2.0/3.x*

Menu Path:	File I Utilities I Import Data I Paradox 2.0/3.x
Description:	Imports data from Paradox files into a new or existing Q&A database.
Procedure:	1. Select Paradox 2.0/3.x from the Import Menu.
	2. Type the name of the Paradox file and press Enter.
	3. Type the name of the Q&A database to receive the data and press Enter.
	4. If the Q&A database does not exist, it will be created with a form design parallel to the file you are importing.
	5. At the Format Spec assign the correct information types to the fields in the new file. After completing the Format Spec, press F10. If the Format Spec contains number, money, date, or time fields, the Global Format Options screen will be displayed. After setting the Global Format Options to your preferences, press F10.
	6. At the Merge Spec, enter the Paradox field numbers into the Q&A fields to receive data. The first field on the top left of the Paradox form is field 1, the field to the right is field 2, and so on down the form.
	7. Press F10 upon completing the Merge Spec.
Notes:	If you are importing into an existing Q&A database, the Format Spec and the Global Format Options screen will not be displayed.
	You cannot import Paradox files with password protection. Remove the protection from the Paradox file prior to beginning the import process.
See Also:	*Merge Spec*
	Format Values for information on the different format identifiers.
	Export to Paradox 2.0/3.x

Import from PFS/Pro File _____

Menu Path: File I Utilities I Import Data I PFS/Pro File

Description: Imports data from PFS File and Professional File databases into a new or existing Q&A database.

Procedure: 1. Select PFS/Pro File from the Import Menu.

2. Type the name of the PFS File or Professional File database and press Enter.

3. Type the name of the Q&A database to receive the data and press Enter.

4. If the Q&A database does not exist, it will be created with a form design parallel to the file you are importing. Any Retrieve Specs, Sort Specs, Print Specs, and Formulas contained in the PFS/Pro File will also be imported.

5. At the Format Spec assign the correct information types to the fields in the new file. After completing the Format Spec, press F10. If the Format Spec contains number, money, date, or time fields, the Global Format Options screen will be displayed. After setting the Global Format Options to your preferences, press F10.

6. At the Merge Spec, enter the PFS or Professional File database field numbers into the Q&A fields to receive data. The first field on the top left of the PFS or Professional File form is field 1, the field to the right is field 2, and so on down the form.

7. Press F10 upon completing the Merge Spec.

Notes: If you are importing into an existing Q&A database, no Retrieve Specs, Sort Specs, Print Specs, or Formulas will be imported. In addition, the Format Spec and the Global Format Options screen will not be displayed.

PFS or Professional File databases with attachment fields are handled differently. To import such a file, allow Q&A to create a new database for the destination. At the Format Spec, Escape from the import process, and redesign the database, adding the attachment fields after all other fields. Now restart the import process, using the original PFS or Professional

File database as the source, and the newly redesigned database as the destination.

See Also: *Merge Spec*

Format Values for information on the different format identifiers.

Redesign a File for information on adding fields to a Q&A database.

_____ *Import from Standard ASCII*

Menu Path: File I Utilities I Import Data I Standard ASCII

Description: Imports a Standard ASCII file into an existing Q&A database. The Standard ASCII file format separates each record onto its own line (delimited by carriage return and linefeed), and separates each field from the next with a comma.

Procedure: 1. Select Standard ASCII from the Import Menu.

2. Type the name of the Standard ASCII file and press Enter.

3. Type the name of the Q&A database to receive the data and press Enter.

4. At the Merge Spec, enter the Standard ASCII field numbers into the Q&A fields to receive the data. The first piece of data on each line corresponds to field 1, the piece of data to the right of the first delimiter corresponds to field 2, and so on.

5. Press F10 upon completing the Merge Spec.

6. At the ASCII Options screen set the following options:

Quotes Around Text—YES if textual data is surrounded by quotes, and NO if not. YES is the default.

Field Delimiter—Specify the character used to separate one field from the next. The options are Return, Semicolon, Comma, and Space. Comma is the default.

7. Press F10 upon completion of the ASCII Options screen.

See Also: *Merge Spec*
                  Import from Fixed ASCII
                  Export to Standard ASCII

Link to SQL _____

Menu Path: File | Utilities | Link to SQL

Description: Provides a front-end link to selected SQL (Structured
                  Query Language) database servers to retrieve specific
                  data from an SQL table, merge SQL data into a Q&A
                  database, or manipulate SQL data.

Procedure: 1. Select Link to SQL from the File Utilities Menu.

                  2. At the Link-to-SQL Menu, select the SQL server
                     with which you will be connecting.

Notes: See the information in the Link to SQL supplement
                  provided by Symantec Corporation.

Lock Database _____

Menu Path: File | Design File | Customize Application | Lock Data-
                  base

Description: Allows specific areas of a database to be locked from
                  all users to prevent tampering.

Procedure: 1. Select Lock Database from the Customize Applica-
                     tion Menu.

                  2. Type the name of the database that you want to
                     protect, then press Enter.

                  3. The Database Lock screen has the following op-
                     tions:

                     Password—This Password must be entered when
                        you want to remove the database lock. Remem-
                        bering this Password is the only way you will
                        be able to change the settings on this screen
                        once it is saved.

                     Redesign and Program—Prevents users from
                        being able to redesign the form, program the
                        form, set field navigation, set field templates,
                        set field names, and set format values.

Design/Redesign Reports—Restricts users from creating new reports but allows them to print predefined ones.

Restrict Values—Locks users out of the Restrict Values Spec.

Set Initial Values—Restricts the use of Set Initial Values.

Speed Up Search—Users cannot assign speed up fields.

Set Read only Fields—Lock users out of the Read Only Spec.

Edit Lookup Table—Users cannot edit the Lookup Table.

Define Custom Help—User are not allowed to define custom help.

Set XLookup Password—Users cannot assign or change the XLookup Password.

Change Palette—Prevents users from changing the palette.

Should the Database Lock Be Enabled—This is the master switch for the database lock. This switch allows the lock to be turned off and back on again without changing the above settings.

4. Press F10 to save the current settings.

Notes: This database lock does not require users to enter passwords like Secure a File. Whenever users attempt to access a locked function, they get a warning message that refers them to the Database Administrator.

See Also: *Secure a File* to put password protection on a file.

_____ *Mass Update*

Menu Path: File | Mass Update

Description: Changes information for a group of records in a Q&A database in a single operation, instead of one record at a time. The user specifies which records to change through a Retrieve Spec, and what changes to make through programming statements entered on an Update Spec.

Procedure:

1. Select Mass Update from the File Menu.

2. Type in the name of the Q&A database to update, and press Enter.

3. Fill in the Retrieve Spec to identify those records to update. Optionally, you press F8 and fill in the Sort Spec. Press F10 when complete.

4. Move the cursor to the field to update.

5. Enter the programming statement specifying the changes to be made. If you cannot fit the statement in the space available on the screen, press F6 to invoke the Program Editor. The Program Editor allows up to 32,000 characters of programming to be entered.

6. Repeat steps 4 and 5 for all fields to update.

7. Optionally, press F8 to display the Auto Program Recalc screen. Set the following options on this screen:

   On Record Entry Statements—If you select YES, On Record Entry statements entered through Program Form will be executed prior to the statements entered on the Update Spec. Selecting NO does not execute On Record Entry statements. The default is NO.

   Calculation Statements—If you select YES, programming statements entered through Program Form will be executed after the statements entered on the Update Spec. On Field Entry and On Field Exit programming is not executed. Selecting NO does not execute Program Form statements. The default is NO.

   On Record Exit Statements—If you select YES, On Record Exit statements entered through Program Form will be executed after the statements entered on the Update Spec. Selecting NO does not execute On Record Exit statements. The default is NO.

8. Press F10 when these options have been set.

9. Q&A will display a warning of how many records will be updated, and you have the option to confirm each update individually. If you choose NO, Q&A will update all records without displaying the records for you to confirm each update. If you select YES, Q&A will display each record for you to confirm the update. At each record you have the following options:

Esc—To cancel the update operation.

Shift-F10—to update the current record, and move to the next record for confirmation.

Ctrl-F10—to update this, and all remaining records that meet the retrieve criteria.

F10—to move to the next record without updating the current record.

Valid Keystrokes: Shift-F7—at the Retrieve Spec to recall the most recently used Retrieve Spec for a current session of working with a given database

F6—at the Update Spec to invoke the Program Editor

F8—at the Update Spec to display the Auto Program Recalc screen

Shift-F8—at the Update Spec to save the current Update Spec

Alt-F8—at the Update Spec to list all saved Update Specs

See Also: *Retrieve Spec*

Sort Spec

Programming Chapter for specific information on available programming statements.

Field Editor for information on entering long statements.

Merge Spec

Description: Establishes a relationship between fields from the current file to fields in the external file during multi-file operations such as Import, Export, and Copy Selected Records. It allows you to specify the order of fields during Export, and designate locations for fields that are being imported.

Procedure:
1. The displayed form is of the current file. Move the cursor to the first field for which you want to make a connection.

2. Enter a number in the field that indicates the position of the related field in the external file. For example, if you are importing a file where the Zip Code is the fifth field, you would type a 5 into the Zip Code field on the Merge Spec.

3. Repeat steps 1 and 2 until all fields have the desired relationships with fields in the external file.

4. Press F10 to continue with the operation.

Notes:
If a field is left blank, it has no related field and therefore it will not receive data during an Import, nor will its contents be copied during Copy Selected Records.

If no values are entered on the Merge Spec, the first field will be related to the first field in the external file, the second will be related to the second, and so on. Any remaining fields will have no relationship.

Each field can have a relationship with only one other field, so all numbers on the Merge Spec must be unique.

See Also: *Copy Selected Records*
Export Data
Import Data

Post

Menu Path: File | Post

Description: Moves data from fields in a source database to fields in another database.

Procedure:
1. Select Post from the File Menu.

2. Enter the name of the file you want to post from (this is the SOURCE database).

3. Enter the name of the file you want to post to (this is the TARGET database).

4. On the Retrieve Spec select which records you want to post from the source database.

5. Optionally, press F8 to sort the records that are being posted.

6. Press F10 to continue.

7. The Posting Spec is where you indicate which fields in the source file you want to post to which fields in the target file. Move to each field you want to post, press F7, and set the following options:

Post the Value of the Field—This contains the name of the current field. To post the value of a different field, move to that field and press F7.

Into External Field—This is the name of the field in the external database that you want to post the information into. Press Alt-F7 for a list of field names in the target file.

When the Field—This is the name of the field in the source file that will serve as the matching field. This field is called the PRIMARY key field. Press Alt-F7 for a list of field names in the source file.

Matches the External Field—This is the name of the field in the target file that will serve as the matching field. This field is called the EXTERNAL key field. For each selected record in the source file, this field will be searched for a value that matches the value in the primary key field. When a match is found, the posting operation will be executed. Press Alt-F7 for a list of field names of the indexed (or speed up) fields in the target file. There may only be one unique external key field for each posting operation. Changing this setting will change it for all other fields on the Posting Spec.

Operation—You may indicate one of the following operations:

Replace—The value in the current field will replace the value of the target field.

Add—The value in the current field will be added to the target field. For numbers that means mathematical addition, for text, the values will be concatenated with a space as a separator, and for keyword fields, the values are concatenated with a semicolon as a separator.

Subtract—The value in the current field will be subtracted from the target field.

Multiply—The value in the current field will be multiplied by the value in the target field.

Divide—The value in the current field will be divided into the value in the target field (that is target divided by source).

Then press F7 to save the post specifications for that field.

8. Repeat step 7 until all fields you wish to post have been filled out. The word POST will appear in each field that contains a posting specification.

9. Optionally, press F8 for the Auto Program Recalc screen. The following options can be set:

On Record Entry Statements—YES will execute any On Record Entry programming statements in the target file. This execution will only happen on records that are posted to and it will occur before the fields are posted.

Calculation Statements—YES will execute any calculation programming statements in the target file. This execution will happen only on records that are posted to and it will occur after the fields are posted.

On Record Exit Statements—YES will execute any On Record Exit programming statements in the target file. This execution will happen only on records that are posted to and it will occur after the fields are posted.

10. Press F10 to save the Posting Spec and the Auto Program Recalc screen.

11. Q&A will scan the source database for any records that match the Retrieve Spec. A warning

box will indicate the number of records that are to be posted and ask if you want to verify them individually. YES will prompt you with each matching record in the target file and ask if you want to execute the post. From each record, F10 will continue to the next record without posting, Shift-F10 will post this record and continue to the next, and Ctrl-F10 will update this record and all the following records without stopping again. Answering NO at the warning box will post all fields automatically. Escape will cancel the operation.

Valid
Keystrokes: F7—on the Posting Spec to set a posting specification

F8—on the Posting Spec to set Auto Program Recalc

Shift-F8—to Save the Posting Spec

Alt-F8—to view a list of saved Posting Specs

See Also: *Retrieve Spec* to select the records from the source file.

Sort Spec to sort the records as they are being posted.

Speed Up Searches to index fields in the target file.

Xlookup Functions and Statements in the Programming Chapter for other ways to move information from one file to another.

Print Options, File

See *Print Options* in the General Chapter.

Print Records

Menu Path: File | Print | Print Records

Description: Prints records according to an existing Print Spec. Print Specs may be temporarily modified prior to printing.

Procedure: 1. Select Print Records from the Print Menu.

2. At the list of available Print Specs, select the name of the Print Spec to use. You also have the

option to create a temporary Print Spec that cannot be saved, but will be used immediately for a
one-print run. To do this press Enter, without any
selection.

3. If you choose an existing Print Spec, you have the
option to temporarily modify the Print Spec. Answer Yes to make modifications, or No to begin
printing. If you choose to make modifications, you
will have the chance to change the Retrieve Spec,
Sort Spec, Fields Spec, Print Options, and Page
Definition. Modifying these specs and options is
identical to the process of designing a Print Spec.

4. If you choose to create a temporary Print Spec by
pressing Enter without a selection, then you will
have the chance to complete the Retrieve Spec,
Sort Spec, Fields Spec, Print Options, and Page
Definition. Completing these specs and options is
identical to the process of designing a Print Spec.

See Also: *Design/Redesign a Spec* for information on creating
Print Specs.

Retrieve Spec

Sort Spec

Print Options in the General Chapter.

Define Page in the General Chapter.

Print, File _____

Menu Path: File | Print

Description: Displays the Print Menu, which facilitates the simple
printing of records, mailing labels, or prepared forms.

Procedure: 1. Select Print from the File Menu.

2. The Print Menu contains the following options:

   Design/Redesign a Spec—Creates or modifies a
   Print Spec.

   Print Records—Prints according to an existing
   Print Spec, or according to Retrieve/Sort/Field
   Specs entered at print time.

   Set Global Options—Sets Global Printing Options
   for the File module.

Rename/Delete/Copy a Spec—Renames, deletes or copies an existing Print Spec.

See Also: *Design/Redesign a Spec* for additional information on Print Specs.

Print Records

Set Global Options for information on the available options.

Rename/Delete/Copy a Spec

Program a File

Menu Path: File I Design a File I Program a File

Description: Displays the Program Menu, which accesses commands to program and aid the programming of a Q&A database.

Procedure: 1. Select Program a File from the Design Menu.

2. The Program Menu displays the following options:

Edit Lookup Table—Allows addition to or modification of columns in the built-in Lookup Table of the database.

Program Form—Allows the addition or modification of programming statements.

Field Navigation—Allows the addition or modification of cursor navigation statements.

Read Only Fields—Allows the assignment of fields for protection from being modified during Add Data or Search/Update.

Set Field Names—Allows the assignment of internal field names to use in programming statements, mail merge, IA queries, and report column headings.

See Also: *Edit Lookup Table*

Program Form

Field Navigation

Read Only Fields

Set Field Names

Program Form _____

Menu Path: File I Design File I Program a File I Program Form

Description: Accepts statements that use Q&A's built-in programming constructs, and functions for execution when
adding or updating data.

Procedure: 1. Select Program Form from the Program Menu.

2. Place the cursor in the field to program.

3. Enter the programming statement. If you cannot
fit the statement in the space available on the
screen, press F6 to invoke the Program Editor. The
Program Editor allows up to 32,000 characters of
programming to be entered.

4. Repeat steps 2 and 3 until all necessary fields are
programmed.

5. Optionally, you may press F8 to bring up the On
Record Entry/On Record Exit profile box. Type in
the field number whose programming statement
you would like to execute On Record Entry or On
Record Exit. Press F10 when finished.

6. Press F10 to save the programming.

**Valid
Keystrokes:**   F6—Program Editor

Ctrl-F6—Bypasses menus to go to Add Data

F7—Bypasses menus to go to Search/Update

F8—On Record Entry/On Record Exit Profile Box

See Also: *Programming Chapter* for specific information on
available programming statements.

Field Editor for information on entering long statements.

Protect Macro File _____

See *Protect Macro File* in the Macros and Menus Chapter

Read Only Fields _____

Menu Path: File I Design File I Program a File I Read Only Fields

Description: Locks a field's contents from being edited by a user during Add Data and Search/Update.

Procedure:
1. Select Read Only Fields from the Program Menu.
2. Type the letter "R" into each field you want to make read-only.
3. Press F10 when finished.

Notes: Read-only fields cannot be edited during Add Data or Search/Update. A read-only field value can be modified through programming statements, mass updates, imports, posting, and copy selected records. On Field Entry and On Field Exit programming statements that are in read-only fields will be executed when a user moves over the field.

See Also: *Field Level Security* to make fields read-only for certain users.

Recover Database

Menu Path: File | Utilities | Recover Database

Description: Attempts to recover a damaged database.

Procedure:
1. Select Recover Database from the Utilities Menu.
2. Type the name of the database to recover.
3. The recover confirmation screen suggests making a backup copy of the database prior to recovery. Follow this suggestion if you do not already have a backup copy. Selecting YES will begin the recovery process, and selecting NO will cancel the process. The default option is NO.
4. The progress of the recover operation will be displayed. At the end of the process, a message will indicate whether the recovery was successful or unsuccessful.

Notes: Since the database is recovered in place, if the recovery fails, the resulting file could be more damaged than before. Therefore, it is wise to make a backup copy of the damaged database prior to attempting a recovery.

The recovery process cannot be aborted once it is started. On large files, this process can take time, so

attempt it only when there is little need for using
your computer.

See Also: *Backup Database* for information on making a
backup copy.

Redesign a File _____

Menu Path: File | Design File | Redesign a File

Description: Facilitates modification of an existing Q&A database
including the addition of fields, deletion of fields,
modification of field attributes (i.e., field label, size,
format, or placement on the screen) and the modification of any background characters on the form design.

Procedure: 1. Select Redesign a File from the Design Menu.

2. Type the name of the Q&A database to redesign
and press Enter.

3. Modify the form design as required. All functionality is the same as when a form is designed. The
form appears as it did when it was first designed,
with one exception. Every field is followed by a
two-letter code. This code is Q&A's internal way
of referring to fields. If you move a field, make
sure to move the code along with the field. If you
delete a field, make sure to delete the code as
well. However, when adding fields do not add a
code as this will be done by Q&A when you have
completed the redesign. The code is case sensitive,
therefore use the same capitalization when moving the code for a field.

4. Press F10 when you have finished modifying the
form design.

5. At the Format Spec, modify the field types as required, and press F10 when finished.

6. If you have money, number, date, or time fields,
the Global Format Options screen will appear.
Modify these options as required, and press F10
when finished.

Notes: The letter codes assigned to every field are extremely important to Q&A. These internal codes are the link to your data, therefore, take great care when moving or deleting fields.

If a field is only a single character long, Q&A will assign a single-letter code. The same stipulations apply to single-letter codes as to two-letter codes when redesigning a form.

If you add new text or keyword fields, and you have taught the Query Guide for use with the IA, then a prompt will be displayed asking if you would like to add the new fields to the Query Guide index. Answer YES if you would like to add the new fields, or NO to skip this operation.

During redesigning of a database, if you have ever modified the internal field names through the Set Field Names command, the Field Names Spec will appear to confirm any modifications Q&A has made to the internal names.

See Also: *Design a New File* for additional information on options and keystrokes.

Format Values for information on the different field types.

Teach Query Guide in the Assistant Chapter for information on teaching the Query Guide.

Set Field Names for additional information on the Field Names Spec.

Remove

Menu Path: File | Remove

Description: Removes a group of records from a database.

Procedure: 1. Select Remove from the File Menu.

2. Type the name of the file you want to remove records from and press Enter.

3. The Remove Menu has the following selections:

   Selected Records—Removes records that are selected with a Retrieve Spec.

> **Duplicate Records**—Removes duplicate records. You can select which fields designate a duplicate record.
>
> **Duplicate Records to ASCII**—Removes duplicate records as above, but moves those removed records to a separate ASCII file.

See Also: *Remove Selected Records*

             Remove Duplicate Records

Remove Duplicate Records _____

Menu Path: File I Remove I Duplicate Records

             File I Remove I Duplicate Records to ASCII

Description: Removes duplicate records from a database. You can select which fields are checked for duplicate records. If specified, the removed records can be saved in an ASCII file.

Procedure: 1. Choose Duplicate Records or Duplicate Records to ASCII from the Remove Menu.

    2. If you selected Duplicate Records to ASCII, enter the name of the ASCII file to contain the duplicate records.

    3. Type one of the following values into a field on the Duplicate Spec. Records that have matching values in that field will be considered as duplicate:

        D—Records are duplicates if this field matches on two or more records. This match is a case-insensitive match, so the capitalization of the fields does not affect the match.

        DS—Records are duplicates if this field matches on two or more records. This match is case-sensitive, so the fields must match and they must be capitalized in the same way.

    4. Repeat step 3 until all fields necessary to designate duplicates have been marked with D or DS. Press F10 to continue.

    5. The database will be scanned for records with duplicate values in the specified fields. A warning box will appear indicating the number of records

that will be removed, and asking if you want to confirm each remove individually. YES will prompt you with each duplicate record and ask if you want to remove it. From each record, F10 will continue to the next record without removing it, Shift-F10 will remove this record and continue to the next, and Ctrl-F10 will remove this record and all the following records without stopping again. Answering NO at the warning box will remove all duplicate records automatically. Escape will cancel the operation.

Notes: Once removed, a record cannot be recovered.

If you chose Duplicate Records to ASCII, the removed records are saved in a standard ASCII format with quotes around the text and commas between fields.

Q&A must use only indexed fields to designate duplicate records. Consequently, if you use fields on the Duplicate Spec that are not indexed, a temporary index will be created. The creation of this index will slow down the process.

Valid Keystrokes: Shift-F8—saves the Duplicate Spec

Alt-F8—lists saved Duplicate Specs

See Also: *Remove Selected Records*

Using Named Specs in the General Chapter for information on saving and retrieving Duplicate Specs.

Remove Selected Records

Menu Path: File | Remove | Selected Records

Description: Removes records from a database that are selected with a Retrieve Spec.

Procedure:
1. Choose Selected Records from the Remove Menu.

2. Fill in the Retrieve Spec to specify the records that you want to remove. Press F10 to continue.

3. The database will be scanned for the selected records. A warning box will appear indicating the number of records that will be removed, and ask-

ing if you want to confirm each remove individually. YES will prompt you with each record and ask if you want to remove it. From each record, F10 will continue to the next record without removing it, Shift-F10 will remove this record and continue to the next, and Ctrl-F10 will remove this record and all the following records without stopping again. Answering NO at the warning box will remove all selected records automatically. Escape will cancel the operation.

Notes: Once removed a record cannot be recovered.

See Also: *Retrieve Spec* to select the records to remove.

 Remove Duplicate Records

Rename a Print Spec ─────────────────────────

See *Rename/Delete/Copy a Spec*

Rename/Delete/Copy a Spec ──────────────────

Menu Path: File | Print | Rename/Delete/Copy a Spec

Description: Displays the Rename/Delete/Copy Menu, which allows basic "housekeeping" operations on Print Specs.

Procedure: 1. Select Rename/Delete/Copy a Spec from the Print Menu.

2. The Rename/Delete/Copy Menu displays the following options:

    Rename a Print Spec—Renames an existing Print Spec to a new name in the same database.

    Delete a Print Spec—Deletes an existing Print Spec from the current database.

    Copy a Print Spec—Copies an existing Print Spec to a new name in the same database.

3. Select the operation to perform, and press Enter.

4. Type the name of the Print Spec to rename, delete, or copy, and press Enter.

5. If you chose to rename or copy a Print Spec, type the new name and press Enter.

See Also: *Design/Redesign a Spec* for information on creating Print Specs.

Restrict Values

Menu Path: File | Design File | Customize a File | Restrict Values

Description: Controls data entry to fields by requiring that values meet certain conditions. Those conditions can restrict a field to a range of numbers, a selection of values, or a specific value.

Procedure:
1. Select Restrict Values from the Customize Menu.

2. On the Restrict Spec move to a field you want restricted and enter a restriction expression (see Table 2.7 for valid expressions).

3. Repeat step 2 for each field you want to restrict then press F10.

Table 2.7. Valid Restriction Expressions

Expression	Field must be...
X	Equal to X
=X	Equal to X
/X	NOT equal to X
=	Empty
X; Y; Z	X or Y or Z NOTE: these values can be chosen from a list during data entry.
>X	Greater than X
<X	Less than X
>=X	Greater than or equal to X
<=X	Less than or equal to X
>X..<Y	Greater than X and less than Y
>X..<=Y	Greater than X and less than or equal to Y
<X; >=Y	Less than X OR greater than or equal to Y
?	Any single character
??	Any two characters
s????	Any five-letter word beginning with s
k..	Any word beginning with k
..k	Any word ending with k
..k..	Any word containing k
..a..b..	Any word containing a and b in that order

(continued)

Table 2.7.   **Valid Restriction Expressions** *(continued)*

Expression	Field must be...
/=	Not empty, but you can force Q&A to accept a blank value
!	Not empty, and the record cannot be saved until the field has a value that matches the field restriction

Notes: Whenever a value is entered into a field that does not meet the field restriction, a warning box appears asking for confirmation of the field's value. The user can press Enter to verify the value and continue. To restrict the user from being able to override the warning box, simply precede the field restriction with an exclamation point (!). For example: if a user enters cherry into a field whose restriction is !apple; banana, the user will not be able to leave the field until it contains either apple or banana.

If a field restriction is a list of valid values (e.g., x; y; z) then the values can be viewed during data entry by moving to the field and pressing Alt-F7. At that time the restrictions cannot be edited. The list will appear in alphabetical order.

Examples: See Table 2.8 for sample restrictions.

Table 2.8.   **Sample Restrictions**

Restriction	Valid Entry	Invalid Entry
Apple	Apple	Banana
>5..<9	7	3
..c	Symantec	Paris
..a..b..	Crab Legs	Banana

**Valid
Keystrokes:**   Ctrl-F6—Move directly to Add Data

F7—Move directly to Search/Update

Retrieve Spec

Description: Allows records to be selected from a file. Records can be selected for nearly every process involving a file: reports, copying records, exporting, etc.

Procedure:
1. If you want all the records in the database, leave the Retrieve Spec blank and press F10.

2. To use a saved Retrieve Spec press Alt-F8 and select it from the list. Otherwise, move to each field that holds information you want to retrieve on, and type a valid retrieve expression (see Table 2.9):

Table 2.9.   Valid Retrieve Expressions

Expression	Finds all records where this field is...
Good for all field types	
X	Equal to X
=X	Equal to X
/X	NOT equal to X
=	Empty
/=	NOT empty
X; Y; Z	X or Y or Z
Good for all field types except Yes/No	
>X	Greater than X
<X	Less than X
>=X	Greater than or equal to X
<=X	Less than or equal to X
>X..<Y	Greater than X and less than Y
>X..<=Y	Greater than X and less than or equal to Y
<X; >=Y	Less than X OR greater than or equal to Y
MAX n	One of n maximum values
MIN n	One of n minimum values
Good for text and keyword fields	
?	Any single character
??	Any two characters
s????	Any five-letter word beginning with s
k..	Any value beginning with k
..k	Any value ending with k
..k..	Any value containing k
..a..b..	Any value containing a and b in that order

You may also enter some special retrieval expressions (see Table 2.10):

Table 2.10. Special Retrieval Expressions

Expression	Meaning and Example
..	Finds correctly formatted values such as valid dates.
/..	Finds incorrectly formatted values such as Unknown in a date field.
&	And operator changes semicolons from ORs to ANDs (e.g., &>Jones;..r finds all records where the last name is greater than Jones AND ends in the letter r).
~X	Sounds-like operator finds all records that sound similar to X (e.g., ~Simantek finds Symantec).
\	Finds the literal of the character (e.g., \? finds a question mark, \.\. finds two periods).
]	Used for wildcard searches (e.g.,]????\10\?? in a date field finds all records in October regardless of the year).

3. Repeat step 2 for each field you want to search on.

4. Optionally, press Ctrl-F7 and set the Search Options. If more than one field has a retrieve specification in it, Q&A will assume that you want only records that meet both criteria. You can, however, press Ctrl-F7 and use the Search Options to tell Q&A exactly how to interpret the multiple entries. Change the settings to match the desired outcome (see Table 2.11):

Table 2.11. Retrieve Spec Search Options

Search Option	ANY	ALL
DO	Finds all records that meet any one or more of the retrieval expressions.	Finds only those records that meet all of the retrieval expressions.
DO NOT	Finds all records except those where any one of the retrieval expressions is met.	Finds all records except those that meet all of the retrieval expressions.

5. Optionally, press F8 to sort the selected records.

6. Optionally, press Shift-F8 to save this Retrieve Spec.

7. When finished, press F10 to execute the retrieval of the records.

Notes: You may also enter programming expressions on the Retrieve Spec. These programming expressions will be executed, and the results will be treated as a regular Retrieve Spec expression. You may enter only programming functions, not statements. Below is an example of Retrieve Spec programming:

```
Date of Sale: >{@Date - 7}
```

Notice that the programming function must be enclosed in braces and it can be mixed with other Retrieve Spec operators (=, >, <, >=, <=, etc.). The example selects all records with a Date of Sale within the past seven days.

Examples:

&..s..;..k..	Finds all words that contain both s and k in any order (e.g., sky and kiss).
]????/06/24	Finds all dates that are June 24 of any year.
{Salary+Bonus > 100000}	Finds all records where the total of the Salary field and the Bonus field is greater than 100,000.

Valid Keystrokes: Shift-F8—Save the current Retrieve Spec

Alt-F8—Display list of saved Retrieve Specs

See Also: *Programming Chapter* for more information about built-in Q&A programming functions.

Search/Update

Sort Spec

Using Named Specs in the General Chapter for information on saving and retrieving Retrieve Specs.

Search/Update

Menu Path: File | Search/Update

Description: Retrieves a group of records for viewing and manually editing.

Procedure: 1. Select Search/Update from the File Menu.

2. Enter the path and name of the file you want to update then press Enter.

3. Fill out the Retrieve Spec to select the record or group of records you want to update.

4. Optionally, press F8 for the Sort Spec to sort the records, then press F10.

5. You may see a message indicating that no forms were found that meet the retrieval specification. If you select YES you may change the Retrieve Spec, NO will cancel the operation.

6. When the first record is on the screen you can begin adding to or changing information in the fields. You may press F6 to add more information into a field than will display on screen. In text and keyword fields you will see the 32K Field Editor, in all other fields you will see a 240-character Expand Field area at the bottom of the screen.

7. Optionally, you may press Alt-F6 to view the records in an editable Table View.

8. When the current record is finished, you can press F10 to save it and continue to the next record that was selected through step 3.

9. When you have finished updating records, press Shift-F10 to save the current record and exit the file.

Notes: Search/Update and Add Data are very similar, so you may want to refer to Add Data to do some more things like: Delete a Record, Get Help for a Field, Navigate Around a Record, Print a Record, Save a Record, or View a Field's Restrictions

Valid Keystrokes: Ctrl-Home—Move to first selected record

Ctrl-End—Move to last selected record

Ctrl-F2—Print the current record and all the selected records after it

F2—Print record

F3—Delete record

Alt-F4—Ignore template

Alt-F5—Auto-type the current time

Ctrl-F5—Auto-type the current date

Alt-F6—Go to Table View

Ctrl-F6—Move directly to Add Data

Shift-F6—Define the Table View Spec

F6—Expand the current field

Alt-F7—View restrictions

Shift-F7—Undo changes made to the current record

Ctrl-F8—Reset @Number (see *@Number* in the Programming Chapter)

Shift-F8—Set Calculation Options

F8—Calculate programming statements on this record

Shift-F9—Menu bypass to several Customize and Program Menu choices

F9—Save record and move to previous record

Shift-F10—Save current record and exit

F10—Save current record and continue

See Also:　　*Add Data*

Field Editor

Retrieve Spec

Sort Spec

Table View

Secure a File

Menu Path:　File | Design File | Secure a File

Description:　Controls access rights to a database.

Procedure:　1. Select Secure a File from the Design Menu.

2. Type the name and path of the database you want to secure, then press Enter.

3. The Security Menu has the following options:

　Assign Access Rights—Assigns User IDs and Passwords to individual users of the database. Also controls the type of functions each user can perform on this database.

Field Level Security—Allows up to eight users or groups of users to each have a different view of the database. These views are created by hiding fields and making others read-only.

Declare Sharing Mode—Sets the file sharing mode for Q&A to use while on networks.

Set XLookup Password—Sets a special ID and Password that will allow XLookup statements to access information from other password-protected databases.

See Also: *Assign Access Rights*
                    Field Level Security
                    Declare Sharing Mode
                    Set XLookup Password

Set Field Names

Menu Path: File I Design File I Program a File I Set Field Names

Description: Assigns internal names to fields for use in programming, mail merge, IA queries, and report column headings.

Procedure: 1. Select Set Field Names from the Program Menu.

2. At the Field Names Spec, modify the field names to your satisfaction. Field names are automatically set when a database is first designed. If the field has a label, the label is used as the field name. Since field names must be unique, if duplicate field labels are used, the second field name will have a "1" after the label, the third a "2," and so on. If the field has no field label, a field name such as "F0001," "F0002," and so on is assigned.

3. Press F10 when you are finished.

Notes: The field names set prior to using the IA with a database become the defaults for the basic lesson, Alternate Field Names. Once you have used a database with the IA, the names set here and the names in the *Alternate Field Names* command from the Assistant Chapter are modified independently. However, Q&A

will not allow names to be duplicated in both commands.

During the *Redesign a File* command, if you have ever modified the internal field names, the Field Names Spec will appear to confirm any modifications Q&A has made to the internal names.

Name changes made in Set Field Names are automatically assumed by the Program Spec, any reports, and any saved specs containing programming. Q&A does not change field names used in mail merge documents.

Examples: The following are possible reasons why you might want to modify field names:

a. To give unlabeled fields more descriptive names than the preassigned names.

b. To shorten the assigned field name for easier use in mail merge or programming.

c. To remove characters from the assigned field name that would otherwise be illegal in programming statements (i.e., if a field label, and therefore the field name, was "Owner?" then the question mark (?) would be illegal in programming), or would be interpreted incorrectly in mail merge (i.e., if a field label, and therefore the field name, was "P O Box" then the "P" would be interpreted in a mail merge as the beginning of a printer control code).

See Also: *Redesign a File*

Programming Chapter for information on using field names in programming statements.

Alternate Field Names in the Assistant Chapter for information on its relationship to this command.

Set Global Options

Menu Path: File | Print | Set Global Options

Description: Displays the Global Options Menu, which allows the Print Options and Page Definition default settings to be altered.

Procedure: 1. Select Set Global Options from the Print Menu.

2. The Global Options contains the following options:

   Change Print Options Defaults—Modifies the Print Options for any newly designed Print Specs.

   Change Define Page Defaults—Modifies the Page Definition for any newly designed Print Specs.

   Change Single Form Print Defaults—Modifies the Print Options for printing single forms (i.e., from Add Data or Search/Update).

   Change Single Form Page Defaults—Modifies the Page Definition for printing single forms (i.e., from Add Data or Search/Update).

See Also: *Change Print Options Defaults*

Change Define Page Defaults

Print Options and *Define Page* in the General Chapter.

Design/Redesign a Spec for information on creating Print Specs.

Add Data

Search/Update

Set Initial Values _____

Menu Path: File | Design File | Customize a File | Set Initial Values

Description: Allows default data values to be entered for any field. These values are displayed whenever a new record is added.

Procedure: 1. Select Set Initial Values from the Customize Menu.

2. Type a default value in any of the fields, and press F10 when finished.

Notes: Initial values can include text, dates, and numbers. There are also three special initial values that can be entered on this screen:

@Number—Enters an incremented number into the field for each new record. This is ideal for invoices where @Number can enter the invoice number auto-matically.

@Date—Stamps the field with the current date. This is useful whenever you need to know the date a re-cord was added.

@Time—Stamps the field with the current time. This is useful whenever you need to know the time of day that a record was added.

@Date and @Time work off of the system clock, so if it is not set correctly then the initial values will not be accurate.

See Also: *Add Data*

@Number, *@Date*, and *@Time* in the Programming Chapter.

Set XLookup Password

Menu Path: File I Design File I Secure a File I Set XLookup Pass-word

Description: The XLookup Password provides XLookup com-mands from this database with an ID and Password to use when accessing external password-protected databases.

Procedure: 1. Select Set XLookup Password from the Security Menu.

2. Enter an ID and Password.

3. Press F10 when finished.

Notes: Assigning an XLookup Password does not put pass-word protection on the current database.

If the XLookup command cannot open the external database with this ID and Password, it will try to use the ID and Password of the current user. If that ID is also unsuccessful then the XLookup command will fail.

See Also: *XLookup Functions and Statements* in the Program-ing Chapter to create an XLookup command.

Assign Access Rights to password-protect a database.

Sort Spec

Description: Sorts records for any operation in a database.

Procedure:
1. Press F8 from any Retrieve Spec to display the Sort Spec.
2. Move the cursor to a field on which to base the sort operation.
3. Type in a number representing the level of importance of this field during the sorting process. A field that has a lower number than another field will be sorted first. Follow the number with either the letters AS or DS; AS represents ascending sort (low to high sort of this field), and DS represents descending sort (high to low sort for this field).
4. Repeat steps 2 and 3 until all fields required for the sort operation have codes in them. Press F10 when the Sort Spec is complete.

Notes: The field with the lowest number is the primary sort field. Q&A will sort the records based on this field first. If there are records on which the values in this field are the same, then Q&A will go to the field with the next highest number to determine how to sort these records. This idea cascades to any additional fields selected for sorting. Usually 3 or 4 sort fields is enough to accomplish most sort tasks.

Sorting text fields with numeric data will result in a nonnumerically sorted set of records (i.e., 1, 10, 11, 2, 20, 22, 3, 30, 33, etc.). To sort numeric data, the field type in Format Values must be Number.

Reports do not have Sort Specs. Sorting for reports is specified in the Column/Sort Spec along with other report codes.

**Valid
Keystrokes:** F6—Gives you additional space for entering sort codes

Shift-F8—Saves the current Sort Spec

Alt-F8—Displays a list of the saved Sort Specs

F9—Takes you back to the Retrieve Spec

See Also:	*Retrieve Spec*
	Format Values
	Design/Redesign a Report for information on sorting a report.

_____ *Speed Up Searches*

Menu Path:	File I Design File I Customize a File I Speed Up Searches
Description:	Lets you create "speedy" or indexed fields so database retrieval is faster by keeping track of the first 16 characters of the field in an index file. In addition, unique and nonunique validation can be assigned.
Procedure:	1. Select Speed Up Searches from the Customize Menu.
	2. In the Speed Up Spec, place the cursor in the field that you want to speed up and type one of the following:

S—to speed up retrieval on the field.

SU—to speed up retrieval on the field, and additionally require a unique value (one that doesn't exist in this field on any other record) in the field. If the value is not unique, Q&A will display the error message "This field should be unique. Please verify before continuing."

SE—to speed up retrieval on the field, and additionally require a nonunique value (one that does exist on some other record) in the field. If the value does not exist on another record, Q&A will display the error message "This value has not been entered before. Please verify before continuing."

3. Repeat step 2 for any additional fields you would like to speed up.

4. Press F10 to save the Speed Up Spec.

Notes:	Up to 115 fields can be indexed. The addition of speedy fields will make retrieval of records faster; however, adding records will take slightly longer as

Q&A finds the correct place for the record in the index file.

See Also: *XLookup Functions and Statements* in the Programming Chapter to see how "speedy fields" are used in assisting xlookup statements and functions.

Table View

Description: Allows records to be browsed and edited in a table form. Table View displays 5 fields from up to seventeen records at one time.

Procedure: 1. Press Alt-F6 to display the Table View from any selected record during Search/Update.

2. When an entire field is highlighted you are in browse mode. In browse mode, pressing an arrow key moves you to the next field in the direction of the arrow.

3. To edit a field, move to that field and press F5 to enter the edit mode. If the field value is longer than the column width, then you will need to press F6 to expand the field before you can change its value. Instead of pressing F5, you will also be put into edit mode if you just start typing in a field.

4. To view a record in Form View, you may press Alt-F6 or F10.

5. Press Escape to exit the file.

Notes: When the cursor is on the rightmost column, pressing the right arrow key will scroll the first column off the screen to the left, and display the next field as the rightmost column. If there isn't another field to display, you will be placed in the column that is currently the first column on the screen. Likewise, moving to the left from the leftmost column will scroll the columns to the right and put the previous field in place of the first column. If there is not a previous column, you will be placed in the last column on the screen.

All programming statements are executed in the Table View. Also, field templates and field restrictions are active while in edit mode.

Table View Spec—You may use the Table View Spec to change which fields appear in the Table View. You may exclude some fields and change the order of the others to suit your current needs. The Table View Spec can be changed with the following steps:

a. Press Shift-F6 from either Form View or Table View.

b. Enter a number in each field you want to include on the Table View making sure that all unwanted fields are blank. The number indicates the order in which the fields should be displayed. The numbers do not have to be consecutive, but there cannot be any duplicates. Alternatively, you may press Alt-F8 and select from any saved Table View Specs.

c. Optionally, press Shift-F8 to save the current Table View Spec.

d. Press F10 to view the table with the current settings.

On a network, Q&A does not lock a record until you are in the edit mode on that record.

Valid Keystrokes:

Ctrl-Home—Move to the first record in the table

Ctrl-End—Move to the last record in the table

Ctrl-F2—Print the current record and all the selected records after it

F2—Print record

F3—Delete record

Alt-F4—Ignore template

Alt-F5—Auto-type the current time

Ctrl-F5—Auto-type the current date

F5—Edit field

Alt-F6—Go back to form view

Ctrl-F6—Move directly to Add Data

Shift-F6—Define the Table View Spec

F6—Expand the current field

Alt-F7—View restrictions

Shift-F7—Undo changes made to the current record

F7—Move to the Retrieve Spec

Ctrl-F8—Reset @Number from Edit Mode only (see *@Number* in the Programming Chapter)

Shift-F8—Set Calculation Options from Edit mode only (see *Add Data* for more information)

F8—Calculate programming statements on this record

Shift-F9—Menu bypass to several Customize and Program Menu choices

F9—Save record and move to previous record

Shift-F10—Save current record and exit

F10—Go back to form view

See Also: *Add Data*
       Search/Update

Utilities, File _____

Menu Path: File | Utilities

Description: Displays the File Utilities Menu which accesses commands for importing data, exporting data, backing up databases, recovering damaged databases, and linking to an SQL server.

Procedure: 1. Select Utilities from the File Menu.

2. The Utilities Menu contains the following options:

Link to SQL—Connects to an SQL server.

Import Data—Brings data from one of several supported database formats into a Q&A database.

Export Data—Puts data from Q&A database into one of several supported database formats.

Backup Database—Creates a backup copy of a Q&A database.

Recover Database—Provides database recovery for damaged Q&A databases.

See Also: *Link to SQL*
       Import Data
       Export Data
       Backup Datbase
       Recover Database

3

Report

This chapter describes how to create and print both columnar and cross tab reports using data from Q&A databases. Data from the reports can be summarized with a variety of calculations. Report information can be customized and enhanced to produce impressive output.

Column/Sort Spec

Description: Specifies which fields appear in a columnar report, their sort order, and their placement. This screen also controls which calculations are done, how the columns are formatted, and how they are enhanced.

Procedure: 1. On the Column/Sort Spec, move to a field that should be included in this report.

2. Type a number from 1 to 9999, indicating the order in which this field should appear. The numbers do not have to be consecutive.

3. Optionally, follow the number with one or more of the following Report Organizational Codes (Table 3.1):

Table 3.1. Report Organizational Codes

Code	Meaning	Description
Sorting Codes		
AS	Ascending Sort	Sort values in this column by ascending order.
DS	Descending Sort	Sort values in this column by descending order.
YS	Yearly Sort	Sort values in this column by year, but not by day. This code cannot be used with other sorting codes, and it can only be used with date fields.

(continued)

Table 3.1.   Report Organizational Codes *(continued)*

Code	Meaning	Description
MS	Monthly Sort	Sort values in this column by year and month, but not by day of month. This code cannot be used with other sorting codes, and it can only be used with date fields.

Column Break Codes—Usable only with AS or DS above.

Code	Meaning	Description
CS	Cancel Subcalculations	Cancels subcalculations based on breaks in this column. Also cancels the skipping of a line when the value in this column changes. NOTE: This assumes that the default Format Option, Action on Column Break, is set to Skip Line. If it is set to Don't Skip Line, then CS will cause subcalculations and a line skip.
P	Page Break	Causes a new page to begin each time the value in this sorted column changes. This code only has an effect on sorted columns.
DB	Day Break	Causes column breaks when the day changes. This is only valid in sorted date columns.
MB	Month Break	Causes column breaks when the month changes, and not when the day of the month changes. This code is only valid in sorted date columns.
YB	Year Break	Causes column breaks when the year changes, and not when the month or day of the month changes. This code is only valid in sorted date columns.
AB	Alphabetic Break	Causes column breaks when the first letter of the sorted text value changes.

Miscellaneous Codes

Code	Meaning	Description
R	Repeat Values	Causes values in this sorted column to be repeated each time they appear. This toggles the Global Format Option, Default to Repeating Values. If the setting is YES then the this code will cause this column to stop repeating values.

(continued)

Table 3.1. Report Organizational Codes *(continued)*

Code	Meaning	Description
I	Invisible	Makes a column invisible. Invisible columns may be used for calculations in Derived Columns.
K	Keyword Report	If put in the first column of a report, it causes each individual keyword of the records to become a separate line of the report. This code is only for keyword fields.

4. Optionally, add one or more of the following Column Calculation Codes (Table 3.2):

Table 3.2. Column Calculation Codes

Code	Meaning	Description
T	Total	Prints the total of the numeric or money column at the bottom of the column.
A	Average	Prints the average of the numeric or money column at the bottom of the column.
C	Count	Prints the count of nonempty values at the bottom of the column.
MIN	Minimum	Prints the minimum value from the column at the bottom of the column.
MAX	Maximum	Prints the maximum value from the column at the bottom of the column.
STD	Standard Deviation	Prints the standard deviation from all values in the column at the bottom of the column.
VAR	Variance	Prints the variance from all values in the column at the bottom of the column.

5. Optionally, add one or more of the following Subcalculation Codes (Table 3.3):

Table 3.3. Column Subcalculation Codes

Code	Meaning	Description
ST	Subtotal	Prints column subtotals of numeric or money fields at each break in previously sorted columns.
SA	Subaverage	Prints column subaverages of numeric or money fields at each break in previously sorted columns.

(continued)

Table 3.3.   Column Subcalculation Codes *(continued)*

Code	Meaning	Description
SC	Subcount	Prints column subcounts at each break in previously sorted columns.
SMIN	Subminimum	Prints column subminimums at each break in previously sorted columns.
SMAX	Submaximum	Prints column submaximums at each break in previously sorted columns.
SSTD	Substandard Deviation	Prints column substandard deviations at each break in previously sorted columns.
SVAR	Subvariance	Prints column subvariances at each break in previously sorted columns.

6. Optionally, add one or more of the formatting codes described in the Formatting Codes command.

7. To enhance parts of the report, press Shift-F6. You may also modify column headings, calculation labels, and separators. For more information see the Report Enhancements, Columnar command.

8. Repeat steps 1 through 7 until all columns have been specified.

9. To create calculated columns that are not part of the database, press F8 for Derived Columns.

10. Press F10 to save the Column/Sort Spec.

Notes: All column codes should be separated with commas. This avoids ambiguity.

Subcalculations will occur when values change in sorted columns to the left of the column being calculated. Therefore, the first column of a report cannot have any subcalculations on it. Subcalculations in a column that is also sorted will not be done based on changes to itself.

Valid Keystrokes: Shift-F6—Enhance a column

F8—Create Derived Columns

Ctrl-F9—Assign fonts

See Also: *Derived Columns*
Design/Redesign a Report
Formatting Codes
Report Enhancements, Columnar
Set Format Options, Columnar

_____ *Columnar Global Options*

Menu Path: Report | Set Global Options | Columnar Global Options

Description: Allows options to be set that affect only columnar reports.

Procedure: 1. Select Columnar Global Options from the Global Options Menu.

2. The Columnar Global Options Menu displays the following choices:

   Set Column Headings/Widths—Allows default column headings and column widths to be specified for all reports, new and old, from the current database.

   Set Format Options—Allows the setting of format options of all columnar reports, new and old, from all databases.

   Set Print Options—Allows default Print Options to be set for all new columnar reports from all databases.

   Set Page Options—Allows a default Define Page to be specified for all new columnar reports from all databases.

See Also: *Set Column Headings/Widths*
Set Format Options, Columnar
Set Print Options
Set Page Options

_____ *Copy a Report*

See *Rename/Delete/Copy*

Cross Tab Global Options _____

Menu Path: Report | Set Global Options | Cross Tab Global Options

Description: Allows options to be set that affect only cross tab reports.

Procedure: 1. Select Cross Tab Global Options from the Global Options Menu.

    2. The Cross Tab Global Options Menu displays the following choices:

> **Set Col/Row Headings**—Allows default headings to be specified for the columns and rows for all reports, new and old, from the current database.

> **Set Format Options**—Allows the setting of format options of all cross tab reports, new and old, from all databases.

> **Set Print Options**—Allows default Print Options to be set for all new cross tab reports from all databases.

> **Set Page Options**—Allows a default Define Page to be specified for all new cross tab reports from all databases.

See Also: *Set Col/Row Headings*

    Set Format Options, Cross Tab

    Set Print Options

    Set Page Options

Cross Tab Spec _____

Description: Specifies which fields will appear as the rows and columns in a cross tab report and which field will be summarized. It also specifies the type of summary function to be performed.

Procedure: 1. Move to the field whose data values will appear as row headings, and type ROW. Each unique value in this field becomes a separate row in the cross tab.

2. Move to the field whose data values will appear as column headings, and type COL. Each unique value in this field becomes a separate column in the cross tab.

3. Move to the field whose data you want to summarize and type SUM. The SUM field will be summarized at each intersection, or cell, of the rows and columns. If the summary column is the same as either the ROW or COL column, then separate the two codes with a comma.

4. Optionally, specify the type of calculation to be done on the summary field by using one or more of the following codes (Table 3.4):

Table 3.4. Summary Calculation Codes

Code	Meaning	Description
T	Total	Totals the values of the summary field for each cell of the report.
A	Average	Averages the values of the summary field for each cell of the report.
C	Count	Counts the number of nonempty values in the summary field for each cell of the report.
MIN	Minimum	Prints the minimum value from the summary field for each cell of the report.
MAX	Maximum	Prints the maximum value from the summary field for each cell of the report.
STD	Standard Deviation	Prints the standard deviation from the summary field for each cell of the report.
VAR	Variance	Prints the variance from the summary field for each cell of the report.

If no summary code is specified, Q&A will use a default calculation based on the format of the summary field. If the summary field is a number or money field, Q&A will use a Total calculation. Otherwise, Q&A will use the Count calculation.

5. You may optionally add NS after the ROW or COL code to keep a summary row or column from printing. If the field is also the SUM field, then the NS code must be placed after the ROW or COL field but before the SUM code (e.g., ROW, NS, SUM).

6. You may add formatting codes described in the Formatting Codes command.

7. Optionally, press Shift-F6 to enhance some or all of the fields.

8. Press F8 if you want to specify Derived Fields.

9. Press F7 to specify the Grouping Spec.

10. Press F10 to save the Cross Tab Spec.

Notes: The Grouping Spec is used to group data values from the ROW and COL fields into meaningful collections. It consists of two columns, one for the rows and one for the columns, into which you may enter codes to identify the groupings. The groups can be specified by explicit grouping. For example, WA; OR; CA would group all the western states onto one row or column of the cross tab. You may enter one of the following Predefined Grouping Specifications (Table 3.5):

Table 3.5. Predefined Grouping Specifications

Grouping	Meaning
@All	Groups data by each unique value in the records. This is the default value on the Grouping Spec.
@Alpha	Groups data by the first letter of each value.
@Day	Groups data by each unique day in the records.
@Dom	Groups data by the day of the month regardless of the month or year.
@Dow	Groups data by the day of the week. This produces a maximum of seven groupings (one for each day of the week).
@Interval @I @Interval(N) @I(N)	Groups data into N equal intervals. If you do not specify a specific N, Q&A computes an "ideal" number of intervals to use.
@Month	Groups data by the month of the year, but separates the same month from different years (i.e., Jun 1990 and Jun 1991 are two different groups).
@Moy	Groups data by the month of the year, regardless of the year. This produces a maximum of 12 groups.

(continued)

Table 3.5. Predefined Grouping Specifications *(continued)*

Grouping	Meaning
@Range(X,Y,Z) @R(X,Y,Z)	Groups data into regular ranges. X is the starting number, Y is the size of the range, and Z is the number of ranges.
@Year	Groups data by year. This produces one group for every year in the database.

If you specify a keyword field as the ROW field of the cross tab, Q&A will put each unique keyword as a separate row in the report.

Valid
Keystrokes: Shift-F6—Enhance report

F7—Grouping Spec

F8—Derived Fields

See Also: *Design/Redesign a Report*

Derived Fields

Formatting Codes

Report Enhancements, Cross Tab

_____ *Define Page, Report*

See *Define Page* in the General Chapter.

_____ *Delete a Report*

See *Rename/Delete/Copy*

_____ *Derived Columns*

Description: Allows the creation of columns in a columnar report whose values are calculated from data in fields that exist in the database, other calculated columns, or a combination of both.

Procedure: 1. While designing a report, press F8 from the Column/Sort Spec to display the Derived Columns screen.

2. Type in the Heading for a derived column, then press Enter. To specify a multiline heading, use exclamation points (!) to separate the lines. To specify the width of the column in characters, enter a number before the heading; follow the number with a colon (:). In columns with data that will require multiple lines, you may optionally specify the number of characters that you would like the second and subsequent lines to be indented. Follow the column width number with the number of characters to indent; follow the number with a colon (:).

3. Type a programming expression into the Formula field for the derived column. To use the values from other columns on the report, use their column numbers or field names in the expression. To use the values from fields not on the report, use their field names in the expression.

4. Type the column specification into the Column Spec field for the derived column as you would on the Column/Sort Spec (i.e., ordering, sorting, breaking, formatting, etc.).

5. Repeat steps 2 through 4 for additional Derived Columns. You may have up to 16 Derived Columns in a single report. To access the additional space for Derived Columns, press PgDn.

6. Press F10 when finished.

Notes: You cannot expand the area for the Heading, Formula, or Column Spec.

Derived Columns can reference themselves in their formulas; this is useful for creating running totals. Self-referencing Derived Columns cannot be sorted.

The following list of special Derived Column summary functions are used to include calculations from other columns in the formula for a derived column:

Table 3.6. Derived Column Summary Functions

Function	Description
Grand Summary Functions	
@TOTAL(n)	Grand total of values in column n.
@AVERAGE(n)	Grand average of values in column n.
@COUNT(n)	Grand count of values in column n.
@MINIMUM(n)	Grand minimum of values in column n.
@MAXIMUM(n)	Grand maximum of values in column n.
@CVAR(n)	Grand variance of values in column n.
@CSTD(n)	Grand standard deviation of values in column n.
Subsummary Functions	
@TOTAL(n,m)	Total values in column n on a break in column m.
@AVERAGE(n,m)	Average values in column n on a break in column m.
@COUNT(n,m)	Count of values in column n on a break in column m.
@MINIMUM(n,m)	Minimum of values in column n on a break in column m.
@MAXIMUM(n,m)	Maximum of values in column n on a break in column m.
@CVAR(n,m)	Variance of values in column n on a break in column m.
@CSTD(n,m)	Standard deviation of values in column n on a break in column m.

All the subsummary functions can take one additional parameter if the column on which the break is based (represented by 'm') is a date value. This parameter specifies what type of date break the function should be executed on. Valid options are DB for day break, MB for month break, and YB for year break. For example, to show the average Salary (#3) for each month of the Pay Date (#2), the formula would be @AVERAGE(#3,#2,MB).

Valid Keystrokes: PgUp—Display the previous page of Derived Columns

PgDn—Display the next page of Derived Columns

F9—Return to the Column/Sort Spec

See Also:	*Design/Redesign a Report* for information on creating reports.
	Column/Sort Spec for information on available options.
	Programming Chapter for information on available programming expressions.

Derived Fields _____

Description:	Allows the creation of fields in a cross tab report whose values are calculated from data in fields that exist in the database, other calculated fields, or a combination of both. Derived fields are used for either the row, column, or summary field required for a cross tab report.
Procedure:	1. From the Cross Tab Spec, press F8 to display the Derived Fields screen.
	2. In the Heading field, type the text to display as the heading of this field. To specify a multiline heading, use exclamation points (!) to separate lines.
	3. In the Formula field, type a programming expression for the derived field. If you are referring to fields in the database that are not a part of the report, assign them numbers on the Cross Tab Spec. Alternately, field names may be used in the programming expression.
	4. In the Cross Tab Spec field, type the Cross Tab codes for the derived field. All Cross Tab Spec codes are available.
Valid Keystrokes:	F9—Go back to Cross Tab Spec
See Also:	*Design/Redesign a Report* for information on creating reports.
	Cross Tab Spec for information on available codes.
	Programming Chapter for information on available programming expressions.

Design/Redesign a Report

Menu Path: Report I Design/Redesign a Report

Description: Creates a named columnar or cross tab report. A report is made up of a Retrieve Spec, Print Options, and Define Page options. In addition, a columnar report requires a Column/Sort Spec, and optionally Derived Columns. Likewise, a cross tab report requires a Cross Tab Spec, and optionally Derived Fields and a Grouping Spec.

Procedure:

1. Select Design/Redesign a Report from the Report Menu.

2. Type the name of the Q&A database in which to create the report, and press Enter.

3. Type the name of the report to create, or select for modification a report from list of existing reports.

4. If you are modifying an existing report, continue with the next step. For a new report, select the type of report to create; either Columnar or Cross Tab. Press Enter upon making the selection.

5. At the Retrieve Spec, enter the retrieval criteria to select the records to include on this report. You may press Alt-F8 to choose from a list of saved Retrieve Specs. Press F10 when finished.

6. Depending on the type of report that you are designing or redesigning, a different spec will appear.

   For columnar reports, at the Column/Sort Spec, enter the columnar codes into fields to determine which fields will appear on the report and in what order, the sorting order of the records, the column and field formatting, column calculations, and text enhancements. Optionally, press F8 to display the Derived Columns screen.

   For cross tab reports, at the Cross Tab Spec, specify the row, column, and summary fields. In addition, you may enter summary calculations, formatting codes, alternate headings, and scale factors. Optionally, press F7 to display the

Grouping Spec or F8 to display the Derived
Fields screen.

Press F10 when finished.

7. At the Print Options screen, set the options that
control where and how the report will print. Optionally, press F8 to display the Define Page options. Set the page dimensions, margins, header,
and footer for the report. Press F10 when finished.

8. The report definition has been saved. If you
would like to print the report, answer YES to the
prompt that is displayed, otherwise answer NO.

**Valid
Keystrokes:**   Shift-F6—At the Column/Sort Spec or Cross Tab
Spec, to display the text enhancement and font
screen

F7—At the Cross Tab Spec, to display the Grouping
Spec

F8—At the Cross Tab Spec, to display the Derived
Fields screen

F8—At the Column/Sort Spec, to display the Derived
Columns screen

Alt-F8—At the Retrieve Spec, list all save specs

Shift-F8—At the Retrieve Spec, save the current spec

Ctrl-F9—At the Column/Sort Spec or Cross Tab
Spec, to display the Font Assignment screen

See Also: *Retrieve Spec* in the File Chapter.

Column/Sort Spec for information on defining a columnar report.

Derived Columns for information on creating derived
columns for a columnar report.

Cross Tab Spec for information on defining a cross
tab report.

Derived Fields for information on creating derived
fields for a cross tab report.

Print Options and *Define Page* in the General
Chapter.

Formatting Codes

Description: Codes to change the format Q&A uses to output data for printed reports. These codes do not change the data in your database, but only affect the output of the report.

Procedure:

1. These codes are available at the Column/Sort Spec, Derived Columns screen, Cross Tab Spec, or the Derived Fields screen. Move the cursor to the field requiring formatting for the report.

2. Place the cursor at the end of the code information in the field, and type a comma (,) followed by an F.

3. Type all formatting codes in a single set of parentheses following the F. If you specify more than one formatting code, separate them with commas. Table 3.7 is a list of valid formatting codes:

Table 3.7. Report Formatting Options

Code	Description
JR	Justify right (default for number and money data)
JL	Justify left (default for text)
JC	Justify center
U	Uppercase characters (text or keyword only)
C	Print numbers or money with commas
WC	Print numbers or money without commas
TR	Truncate values that don't fit in space for column (do not wrap values)
Dn	Format date value using the specified format 'n'. The format numbers (1–20) are from *Format Values* in the File Chapter
Hn	Format hour value using the specified format 'n'. The format numbers (1–3) are from *Format Values* in the File Chapter
Nn	Format as a numeric value with 'n' (1–7) decimal digits
M	Treat as money value
T	Treat as text value

4. Repeat steps 1 through 4 for all fields requiring formatting.

See Also: *Column/Sort Spec* for information on available columnar report codes.

Derived Columns for information on creating calculated columns for columnar reports.

Cross Tab Spec for information on available cross tab report codes.

Derived Fields for information on creating calculated fields for cross tab reports.

Format Values in the File Chapter for information on the different date and time formats available.

Print a Report

Menu Path: Report | Print a Report

Description: Prints a columnar or cross tab report that has been defined with the Design/Redesign a Report command. Also, a temporary report can be created and printed.

Procedure: 1. Select Print a Report from the Report Menu.

2. Type the name of the Q&A database from which you want to print a report, and press Enter.

3. Type the name of the report to print, or select it from the list of existing reports. If you want to create and print a temporary report, just press Enter without making a selection.

4. If you are printing an existing report, indicate whether you would like to make any temporary changes to the report. If you select YES, continue with the next step; if you select NO, the report will print with all the specified options that are saved with the report. If you are creating a new report, select the type of report, either Columnar or Cross Tab, and press Enter.

5. At the Retrieve Spec, enter or change the retrieval criteria to select the records to include on this report. You may press Alt-F8 to choose from a list of saved Retrieve Specs. Press F10 when finished.

6. Depending on the type of report that you are creating or printing, a different spec will appear.

    For Columnar Reports, at the Column/Sort Spec, enter or change the columnar codes into fields to determine which fields will appear on the report and in what order, the sorting order of the records, the column and field formatting, column calculations, and text enhancements. Optionally, press F8 to display the Derived Columns screen.

For Cross Tab Reports, at the Cross Tab Spec specify or change the row, column, and summary fields. In addition, you may enter summary calculations, formatting codes, alternate headings, and scale factors. Optionally, press F7 to display the Grouping Spec.

7. At the Print Options screen, set the options that control where and how the report will print. Optionally, press F8 to display the Define Page options. Set the page dimensions, margins, header, and footer for the report. Press F10 to print the report.

Notes: All changes made to a report through Print a Report will be lost as soon as the report is printed.

Valid Keystrokes: Shift-F6—At the Column/Sort Spec or Cross Tab Spec, to display the Text Enhancement and Font Screen

F7—At the Cross Tab Spec, to display the Grouping Spec

F8—At the Cross Tab Spec, to display the Derived Fields screen

F8—At the Column/Sort Spec, to display the Derived Columns screen

Alt-F8—At the Retrieve Spec, list all save specs

Shift-F8—At the Retrieve Spec, save the current spec

Ctrl-F9—At the Column/Sort Spec or Cross Tab Spec, to display the Font Assignment screen

See Also: *Retrieve Spec* in the File Chapter.

Design/Redesign a Report to create new reports.

Column/Sort Spec for information on defining a columnar report.

Derived Columns for information on creating derived columns for a columnar report.

Cross Tab Spec for information on defining a cross tab report.

Derived Fields for information on creating derived fields for a cross tab report.

Print Options and *Define Page* in the General Chapter.

Using Named Specs in the General Chapter to view saved Retrieve Specs.

Print Options, Columnar _____

See *Print Options* in the General Chapter.

Print Options, Cross Tab _____

See *Print Options* in the General Chapter.

Rename a Report _____

See *Rename/Delete/Copy*

Rename/Delete/Copy _____

Menu Path:	Report I Rename/Delete/Copy
Description:	Displays the Rename/Delete/Copy Menu, which allows basic "housekeeping" operations on reports.
Procedure:	1. Select Rename/Delete/Copy from the Report Menu.

2. The Rename/Delete/Copy Menu displays the following options:

Rename a Report—Renames an existing Report to a new name in the same database.

Delete a Report—Deletes an existing Report from the current database.

Copy a Report—Copies an existing Report to a new name in the same database.

3. Select the operation to perform and press Enter.

4. Type the name of the report to rename, delete, or copy, and press Enter.

5. If you chose to rename or copy a report, type the new name and press Enter.

See Also: *Design/Redesign a Report* for information on creating reports.

_____ *Report Enhancements, Columnar*

Description: Allows the modification and enhancement of column headings, calculation labels, or separator lines.

Procedure: 1. At the Column/Sort Spec, move to the field whose heading, calculation label, or separator line you would like to modify or enhance and enter one or more of the applicable codes shown in Table 3.8:

Table 3.8.   Columnar Report Enhancements

Code	Description
Summary Calculation Codes	
TL	Enhance/Modify the TOTAL label.
AL	Enhance/Modify the AVERAGE label.
CL	Enhance/Modify the COUNT label.
MINL	Enhance/Modify the MINIMUM label.
MAXL	Enhance/Modify the MAXIMUM label.
STDL	Enhance/Modify the STANDARD DEVIATION label.
VARL	Enhance/Modify the VARIANCE label.
Subcalculation Codes	
STL	Enhance/Modify the SUBTOTAL label.
SAL	Enhance/Modify the SUBAVERAGE label.
SCL	Enhance/Modify the SUBCOUNT label.
SMINL	Enhance/Modify the SUBMINIMUM label.
SMAXL	Enhance/Modify the SUBMAXIMUM label.
SSTDL	Enhance/Modify the SUBSTANDARD DEVIATION label.
SVARL	Enhance/Modify the VARIANCE label.
Year/Month Codes	
YTL	Enhance/Modify the YEAR TOTAL label.
YAL	Enhance/Modify the YEAR AVERAGE label.
YCL	Enhance/Modify the YEAR COUNT label.
YMINL	Enhance/Modify the YEAR MINIMUM label.
YMAXL	Enhance/Modify the YEAR MAXIMUM label.

(continued)

Table 3.8.   Columnar Report Enhancements *(continued)*

Code	Description
YSTDL	Enhance/Modify the YEAR STANDARD DEVIATION label.
YVARL	Enhance/Modify the YEAR VARIANCE label.
MTL	Enhance/Modify the MONTH TOTAL label.
MCL	Enhance/Modify the MONTH COUNT label.
MMINL	Enhance/Modify the MONTH MINIMUM label.
MMAXL	Enhance/Modify the MONTH MAXIMUM label.
MSTDL	Enhance/Modify the MONTH STANDARD DEVIATION label.
MVARL	Enhance/Modify the MONTH VARIANCE label.

Separator Codes

Code	Description
HS	Enhance/Modify heading separator lines.
SL	Enhance/Modify a single separator line used for subcalculation breaks.
DL	Enhance/Modify a double separator line used for grand totals.

Column Heading Codes

Code	Description
H	Enhance/Modify the column heading.

Text in parentheses immediately following the code will be used in place of the default text (i.e., in the Salary field, H (Monthly Wages) will replace the heading of Salary with Monthly Wages).

2. To enhance the label, heading, or separator, move to the appropriate code. To enhance the data move to the column number. Press Shift-F6 to display the Text Enhancements and Font Menu, and select the type of enhancement to apply.

3. Repeat steps 1 and 2 for each field.

Notes: Labels for grand calculations (i.e., T for grand total, A for grand average, etc.) must appear in the first columns spec. To modify/enhance the label for a subcalculation, or a year/month calculation, the code must be placed in the column spec which causes the break.

Examples: In an employee database, to create a report with total bonus dollars and average salary dollars per department where the TOTAL label and the AVERAGE label are modified and boldfaced, the column spec would be as follows:

Department: 1, as, **sal(Average by Dept), tl(Total Bonuses)**

Salary: 2,sa

Bonus: 3,t

See Also: *Column/Sort Spec* for information on columnar report codes.

Text Enhancements and Fonts Menu in the General Chapter.

_____ *Report Enhancements, Cross Tab*

Description: Allows the modification and enhancement of column/row/summary headings, calculation labels, or separator lines. Data may also be enhanced.

Procedure: 1. At the Cross Tab Spec, move to the field whose heading, calculation label, or separator line you would like to modify or enhance and enter one or more of the following applicable codes (Table 3.9):

Table 3.9. Cross Tab Report Enhancements

Code	Description
Summary Calculation Codes	
TL	Enhance/Modify the TOTAL label.
AL	Enhance/Modify the AVERAGE label.
CL	Enhance/Modify the COUNT label.
MINL	Enhance/Modify the MINIMUM label.
MAXL	Enhance/Modify the MAXIMUM label.
STDL	Enhance/Modify the STANDARD DEVIATION label.
VARL	Enhance/Modify the VARIANCE label.
Separator Codes	
HS	Enhance/Modify separator lines for the report's main title.
SL	Enhance/Modify the single separator line between a column's heading and data.
DL	Enhance/Modify the double separator line between the data and the summary calculations.

(continued)

Table 3.9.   Cross Tab Report Enhancements *(continued)*

Code	Description
Column Heading Codes	
H	Enhance/Modify the row, column, or summary heading.
SH	Enhance the subheading of the column or row field. This heading is from the actual data, and cannot be changed.

Text in parentheses immediately following the code will be used in place of the default text (i.e., in the Salary field, H (Monthly Wages) will replace the heading of Salary with Monthly Wages).

2. To enhance the label, heading, or separator, move to the appropriate code. To enhance the data in the field move to the COL, ROW, or SUM code. Press Shift-F6 to display the Text Enhancements and Font Menu, and select the type of enhancement to apply.

3. Repeat steps 1 and 2 for each field.

Notes: You may also enhance grouped rows or columns from the Grouping Spec. Follow the above directions, but highlight the appropriate grouping for enhancement. If you want to enhance only certain rows or columns in the grouping, list the data values to enhance preceded by a percent sign (%).

See Also: *Cross Tab Spec* for information on available cross tab report codes.

Text Enhancements and Fonts Menu in the General Chapter.

Set Col/Row Headings

Menu Path: Report I Set Global Options I Cross Tab Global Options I Set Col/Row Headings

Description: Sets default column, row, and summary headings for all cross tab reports, new and old, from the current database.

Procedure: 1. Select Set Col/Row Headings from the Cross Tab Global Options Menu.

2. To give a field a new default heading, enter the heading into the field. You may separate a long heading onto several lines by typing an exclamation point (!) to separate the lines.

3. Repeat step 2 until all fields have the desired default headings.

4. Press F10 to continue.

See Also: *Set Column Headings/Widths* to set column headings for columnar reports.

_____ *Set Column Headings/Widths*

Menu Path: Report I Set Global Options I Columnar Global Options I Set Column Headings/Widths

Description: Sets default column headings and column widths for all reports, new and old, from the current database.

Procedure: 1. Select Set Column Headings/Widths from the Columnar Global Options Menu.

2. To specify the width of a column, enter a number from 1 to 80 representing the number of characters wide the column should be. You may also specify the width in inches or centimeters. To use inches, follow the number of inches with a quote mark (''); to use centimeters, follow the number with the letters cm.

3. To give a column a new default heading, enter the heading into the field. You may separate a long heading onto several lines by typing an exclamation point (!) to separate the lines. If you are also specifying a column width for this column, separate the width from the heading with a colon (:) (e.g., 12:New Heading).

4. You may optionally indent the second and following lines of a lengthy field by adding another number after the column width. You may only specify indentation if the column width is also specified. The number is the width in characters of

the indentation. Again, a colon is used to separate the different parts of the entry.

5. Repeat steps 2 through 4 until all fields have the desired default settings.

6. Press F10 to continue.

Notes: By default a column width will adjust to fit the longest value for the current report or the column heading, whichever is longer. Text values that are longer than the column width will wrap to the next line. Numeric values that are longer than the specified column width will appear as asterisks. Column headings that are longer than the column width will be truncated.

If a column heading begins with a number you must precede it with a backslash (\) to distinguish it from a column width or indentation value (e.g., 20:\9th Region Totals). Also, if a column heading needs to contain an exclamation point, you should precede it with a backslash (e.g., Total Sales\! becomes Total Sales!). Likewise, if you want a backslash character in the heading, precede it with another backslash (e.g., Files in!C:\\QA4\\FILES becomes a two-line heading with C:\QA4\FILES as the second line).

Examples:

```
20:2:Review!Comments
```
                              Review
                              Comments
The above column heading   -
becomes the column to the   John is a wonderful
right.   worker. He is
                              very productive.

See Also: *Set Col/Row Headings* to set column and row headings for cross tab reports.

Set Format Options, Columnar

Menu Path: Report | Set Global Options | Columnar Global Options | Set Format Options

Description: Allows the setting of format options of all columnar reports, new and old, from all databases.

Procedure: 1. Select Set Format Options from the Columnar
                     Global Options Menu.

2. Set the following options as desired:

   # of Spaces Between Columns—This controls the
   amount of horizontal space between the columns of a report. The selected number represents the number of character spaces. Variable
   is the default; it will use between 2 and 9
   spaces to make the most effective use of the
   printed page.

   Default to Repeating Values—When report columns are sorted, only the first occurrence of
   each separate value in the sorted column will
   be printed. Changing this setting to YES will
   change the default so that all occurrences of
   each separate value in sorted columns will be
   printed. This setting is just a default toggle. It
   can be changed for each column individually
   by using the R parameter on the Column/Sort
   Spec.

   Action on Blank Value—This setting controls
   what happens when number or money fields
   are left blank. The default is Leave Blank.

      Print 0—This will change the blank to a zero
      value.

      Leave Blank—This will leave the blank value.

   Action on Column Break—When report columns
   are sorted, a line is skipped between each
   unique value in the sorted column. Changing
   this setting to Don't Skip Line will change the
   default so that a line is not skipped between
   each separate value in sorted columns. The
   blank line is where column subcalculations are
   printed. Consequently, you may get peculiar results with preexisting reports after changing
   this setting. This setting is just a default toggle.
   It can be changed for each column individually
   by using the CS parameter on the Column/
   Sort Spec.

See Also: *Column/Sort Spec*

Set Format Options, Cross Tab _____

Menu Path: Report I Set Global Options I Cross Tab Global Options I Set Format Options

Description: Allows the setting of format options of all cross tab reports, new and old, from all databases.

Procedure: 1. Select Set Format Options from the Cross Tab Global Options Menu.

2. Set the following options as desired:

# of Spaces Between Columns—This controls the amount of horizontal space between the columns of a report. The selected number represents the number of character spaces. Variable is the default; it will use between 2 and 9 spaces to make the most effective use of the printed page.

Action on Blank Value—This setting controls what appears as the column or row heading when money or numeric fields contain blank values. The default is set to leave the column or row heading blank.

Print 0—This will change the blank column or row heading to a zero value.

Leave Blank—This will leave the column or row heading blank.

Show "No Entry" Columns/Rows—Whenever a column or row in a cross tab report has no data, The default setting is to not show those columns. Changing this setting to YES will include the columns or rows that have no data.

See Also: *Cross Tab Spec*

Set Global Options _____

Menu Path: Report I Set Global Options

Description: Allows global settings to be specified for Print Options, Define Page, Format Options, and Column Headings and Widths.

Procedure:	1. Select Set Global Options from the Report Menu.
	2. Enter the name of the file for which you want to set the options. Some options affect all reports from one database, while others affect all reports from all databases.
	3. The Global Options Menu contains the following choices:

        Columnar Global Options—Allows options to be set that affect only columnar reports.

        Cross Tab Global Options—Allows options to be set that affect only cross tab reports.

| **See Also:** | *Columnar Global Options* |
| | *Cross Tab Global Options* |

Set Page Options

Menu Path:	Report I Set Global Options I Columnar Global Options I Set Page Options
	Report I Set Global Options I Cross Tab Global Options I Set Page Options
Description:	Sets default Define Page settings for all new reports from all databases. Preexisting reports will not be affected by any changes made here.
Procedure:	1. Select Set Page Options from the Columnar Global Options Menu or the Cross Tab Global Options Menu.
	2. Change the settings as desired on the Define Page screen, then press F10 to save them as the defaults for all new reports.
See Also:	*Define Page* in the General Chapter.

Set Print Options

| **Menu Path:** | Report I Set Global Options I Columnar Global Options I Set Print Options |
| | Report I Set Global Options I Cross Tab Global Options I Set Print Options |

Description: Sets default Print Options for all new reports from all databases. Preexisting reports will not be affected by any changes made here.

Procedure:
1. Select Set Print Options from the Columnar Global Options Menu or the Cross Tab Global Options Menu.
2. Change the settings as desired on the Report Print Options screen, then press F10 to save them as the defaults for all new reports.

See Also: *Print Options* in the General Chapter.

4

Write

The details of Q&A's word processor are discussed in this chapter. The word processor allows you to create, save, and print word processing documents. Documents can be as simple as letters, or as complicated as this book. Headers, footers, fonts, and many other advanced word processing functions are available.

Q&A word processing documents can also merge information from Q&A databases to create form letters or mailing labels.

Align Text

Menu Path: Write | Type/Edit

Description: Controls justification and spacing of text in a document. Lines can be left, center, or right justified. Additionally, temporary margins and line spacing can be set.

Procedure: 1. Press F8 from the Type/Edit screen to display the Options Menu.

2. Select Align Text to display the submenu with the following items:

Left—Places the text on the selected line as far to the left as possible.

Center—Places the text on the selected line centered between the left and right margins.

Right—Places the text on the selected line as far to the right as possible.

Temp Margins—Sets temporary margins for blocks of text that require different margins than the rest of the document.

Single Space—Leaves no blank lines on the screen between lines of the document from the cursor on.

Double Space—Leaves one blank line on the
screen between lines of the document from the
cursor on.

Triple Space—Leaves two blank lines on the
screen between lines of the document from the
cursor on.

See Also: *Set Temporary Margins*

Assign Fonts ⎯⎯⎯⎯⎯⎯⎯⎯⎯⎯⎯⎯⎯⎯⎯⎯

See *Font Assignments* in the General Chapter.

Block Operations ⎯⎯⎯⎯⎯⎯⎯⎯⎯⎯⎯⎯⎯⎯

Menu Path: Write I Type/Edit

Description: Operations on selected lines, paragraphs, or pages of
text (blocks) that allow manipulation such as moving,
and copying.

Procedure: 1. Place the cursor on the beginning or ending character of the text block to manipulate.

2. Press F8 from the Type/Edit screen to display the
Options Menu.

3. Select Block Operations to display the submenu
with the following commands:

Copy—Copy a block of text to another place in
the document.

Move—Move a block of text to another place in
the document.

Delete—Delete a block of text from the document.

Copy to File—Copy a block of text to a new Q&A
Write file.

Move to File—Move a block of text to a new
Q&A Write file.

Enhance—Enhance or font a block of text.

Print—Print a block of text.

Capitalize—Use all capital letters for the block of
text.

    Lowercase—Use all lowercase letters for the block of text.

    Title—Use capital letters for the first character of all nonprepositions and acronyms.

4. Select the block operation to perform.

5. If you are enhancing a block, at the Text Enhancements and Fonts Menu select the type of enhancement or font to apply. Optionally, you may select the Assign Fonts option.

6. Use the arrow keys to highlight the block, and press F10.

7. If you are moving or copying a block within the same document, move the cursor to the position to place the selected text. If you are moving or copying a block to another file, enter the name of the new Q&A file to receive the selected text.

Notes: To select a text block, you may use the same keys discussed in the Type/Edit command. In addition, if you press an alphabetic, numeric, or punctuation character while selecting text for an operation, all text from the cursor through the next occurrence of that character will be selected. For example, Pressing Enter will select from the cursor through the next carriage return.

A copy of the highlighted text is kept in memory if you are copying, moving, or deleting the text. This text can be recalled via the Restore command.

If you are printing a block, the printer installed for the document will be used. None of the fonts and text enhancements will be printed.

**Valid
Keystrokes:** F5—At the Type/Edit screen to copy a block

Shift-F5—At the Type/Edit screen to move a block

F3—At the Type/Edit screen to delete a block

Ctrl-F5—At the Type/Edit screen to copy a block to a file

Alt-F5—At the Type/Edit screen to move a block to a file

Shift-F6—At the Type/Edit screen to enhance or font a block

Ctrl-F2—At the Type/Edit screen to print a block

See Also: *Text Enhancements and Fonts Menu* in the General Chapter.

Restore for information on restoring text.

Calculate _____

Menu Path: Write | Type/Edit

Description: Performs mathematical functions on rows or columns of numbers in the document.

Procedure:
1. On the Type/Edit screen position the cursor to the right of the last number in the row, or on the bottom number in the column you want to calculate.

2. Press F8 to display the Options Menu. Select Other Options and press Enter.

3. From the Other Options Submenu, select Calculate and press Enter.

4. The selected row or column of numbers should be highlighted. If the desired numbers are not highlighted, press Escape, and start again with step 1. Otherwise, at the Calculation Menu, press the letter corresponding to the desired calculation:

   Total—Calculates the sum of the highlighted numbers.

   Average—Calculates the average of the highlighted numbers.

   Count—Counts the highlighted numbers.

   Multiply—Calculates the product of all the highlighted numbers.

   Divide—Calculates the quotient of the two numbers closest to the cursor; the rightmost two numbers in a row calculation, and the bottom two numbers in a column calculation. In a row, the quotient is the left number divided by the right number, and in a column it is the top number divided by the bottom number.

5. Position the cursor where you want the result typed, and press F10.

Notes: You may also execute this command by pressing Alt-F9 from the Type/Edit screen.

Capitalize Block

See _Block Operations_

Change Import Defaults

Menu Path: Write I Utilities I Set Global Options I Change Import Defaults

Description: Changes the default Define Page options in effect for documents imported using the Get Document command.

Procedure: 1. Select Change Import Defaults from the Global Options Menu.

2. Define the page to your preference for ASCII, Wordstar, or Lotus documents that are imported into Q&A.

3. Press F10 to save the new defaults.

See Also: _Get_ for information on importing the specified document formats.

Define Page in the General Chapter.

Change Page Defaults to set the default page options for new Q&A Write documents.

Change Print Defaults to set the default print options for new and imported documents.

Change Page Defaults

Menu Path: Write I Utilities I Set Global Options I Change Page Defaults

Description: Changes the default Define Page options in effect for new documents.

Procedure:	1. Select Change Page Defaults from the Global Options Menu.
	2. Define the page to your preference.
	3. Press F10 to save the new defaults.
See Also:	*Define Page* in the General Chapter.
	Change Print Defaults to set the print options for new and imported documents.

Change Print Defaults _____

Menu Path:	Write I Utilities I Set Global Options I Change Print Defaults
Description:	Changes the default Print Options in effect for new or imported documents.
Procedure:	1. Select Change Print Defaults from the Global Options Menu.
	2. Modify the Print Options screen to your preference.
	3. Press F10 to save the new options.
See Also:	*Print Options* in the General Chapter.
	Change Page Defaults to modify the default page definition for new documents.
	Change Import Defaults to modify the default page definition for documents imported via the Get command.

Clear _____

Menu Path:	Write I Clear
Description:	Clears the current document from memory, and displays a blank Type/Edit screen for creation of a new document.
Procedure:	1. Select Clear from the Write Menu. A blank Type/Edit screen will appear for creation of a new document. The text "New Document" will appear in the bottom left corner of the screen.

See Also: *Get* for information on loading a document into
memory.

_____ *Copy a Document*

See *DOS File Facilities* in the Utilities Chapter.

_____ *Copy Block*

See *Block Operations*

_____ *Copy Block to File*

See *Block Operations*

_____ *Define Page, Write*

See *Define Page* in the General Chapter.

_____ *Delete a Document*

See *DOS File Facilities* in the Utilities Chapter.

_____ *Delete Block*

See *Block Operations*

_____ *Documents*

Menu Path: Write | Type/Edit

Description: Accesses the 12 most recently viewed or edited documents, gets a user-specified document, or inserts a
user-specified document into the current document.

Procedure: 1. Press F8 from the Type/Edit screen.

2. At the Options Menu select the Documents option
to display the following items on the submenu:

Previously Accessed Documents (1-9, A-C)—The 12 most recently accessed documents are kept in the order in which they were accessed, most recent being first. Enter a 1 to select the most recently accessed document, 2 for the next one, and so on. If 12 documents have not been accessed, the list will be shorter, and may even be empty.

Insert a Document—Inserts a document into the current document at the cursor position.

Get a Document—Loads a document into Q&A Word Processor for editing.

Notes: Previously accessed documents are saved across sessions of Q&A. Therefore, if during one session of Q&A you access a document, then after exiting you return for a second session, the list will contain the document previously accessed. If during the first session the list already contained 12 documents, the oldest document will be removed from the list to make room for the newly accessed document.

See Also: *Insert a Document* for information on placing another document in the current document.

Get for information on loading a document.

DOS Facilities _____

See *DOS File Facilities* in the Utilities Chapter.

Draw _____

Menu Path: Write I Type/Edit

Description: Allows you to draw lines and boxes in the document.

Procedure: 1. Press F8 from the Type/Edit screen to display the Options Menu.

2. Select Lay Out Page and press Enter.

3. From the Lay Out Page Submenu select Draw and press Enter.

4. Use the arrow keys on the numeric keypad to draw lines. The 7,9,1 and 3 keys on the keypad

will draw diagonal lines in the appropriate direction. To draw double lines, hold down the shift key while using the arrow keys or set the Numlock key and then use the arrow keys.

5. Press F6 to lift the pen so that the cursor can be moved without drawing. Press F6 to put the pen back down.

6. Press F8 to erase any lines that were drawn in error. Press F8 to begin drawing again.

7. Press F10 when finished.

Notes: Not all printers can print the characters used for drawing the lines or boxes. Consequently, the printed document may substitute dashes (-) and pipe symbols (¦) for the lines of the box and plus signs (+) for the corners and intersections.

Valid Keystrokes: F6—Lift or put down the drawing pen

F8—Begin or end erasing lines

_____ *Edit Header and Footer*

Menu Path: Write | Type/Edit

Description: Allows you to type information that will appear in the top or bottom margin on each page of the document.

Procedure: 1. Press F8 from the Type/Edit screen to display the Options Menu.

2. Select Lay Out Page and press Enter.

3. From the Lay Out Page Submenu select either Edit Header or Edit Footer and press Enter.

4. Type the information that you want to appear in the header or footer.

5. Optionally, press F8 to display the Options Menu. Those options not available will be grayed out. You may also enhance the text by pressing Shift-F6.

6. Press F10 when finished editing.

Notes: Headers and footers are printed in the top and bottom margins of documents respectively, so their size will vary depending on the size of the top and bottom margins on the Define Page screen. Headers and footers will be printed on the first page unless specified differently on the Define Page screen.

To put a page number in either the header or footer type a pound sign (#) where the page number should appear. If you want a literal pound sign in the header or footer, precede it with a backslash (\).

Example: The header: Results in:
Page \##   Page #1

Valid Keystrokes: Shift-F6—Enhance text

F8—Options

See Also: *Options Menu*

Define page in the General Chapter.

Enhance Block

See *Block Operations*

Export a Document

Menu Path: Write I Utilities I Export a Document

Description: Exports Q&A documents to several other formats.

Procedure: 1. Select Export a Document from the Write Utilities Menu.

2. Select the document format to which you are trying to export. The following is a list of available formats and the versions supported:

ASCII

Document ASCII

Macintosh ASCII

DCA

WordStar—Versions 3.3, 3.31, 3.45, 4.0, 5.0, 5.5

WordPerfect—Versions 5.0, 5.1

Microsoft Word—Versions 3.0, 3.1, 4.0, 5.0

MultiMate—Versions 3.3, 3.6, 3.7, 4

PFS: Write—Version C

Professional Write—Versions 1.0, 2.0, 2.1

PFS: First Choice—Versions 1.0, 2.0

3. Type the name of the Q&A file you want to export and press Enter.

4. Type a new name for the document in its new format, and press Enter.

See Also: *Import a Document*

Get

Menu Path: Write | Get

Description: Loads an existing document into the Type/Edit screen for editing.

Procedure:
1. Select Get from the Write Menu and skip to step 4, or press F8 from the Type/Edit screen to display the Options Menu.

2. Select the Documents option to display the Documents Submenu.

3. Select Get a Document.

4. Type the name of the document to get, and press Enter.

5. If the file is not recognized as a Q&A Write document, the Import Document Menu will be displayed. Select one of the following options:

ASCII—Files containing only ASCII characters, with no formatting, or embedded codes in the text. All carriage returns are imported.

Special ASCII—Files containing only ASCII characters, with no formatting, or embedded codes in the text. Carriage returns not at the end of paragraphs or blank lines are removed.

WordStar—Documents created with the Wordstar word processing package.

Lotus 1-2-3 or Symphony—Spreadsheets created with either Lotus or Symphony. The Lotus

Range Spec will be displayed. You may select an absolute or predefined range. The selected range of the spreadsheet is imported at the cursor with carriage returns at the end of each row.

6. The document will be loaded into the Type/Edit screen for editing.

Notes: If you have set the Default Import Type for one of the four possible formats using the Set Editing Options, the Import Document Menu will not be displayed, and the document will be automatically imported in the selected format.

You cannot save the document in the format from which it was originally imported, except for ASCII.

See Also: *Type/Edit* for information on editing the document once it is loaded.

Import a Document for additional formats to import.

Documents for additional ways to load documents for editing.

Save as ASCII for information on saving a document in an ASCII format.

Set Editing Options for information on setting the default document import type.

Go to Page/Line _____

Menu Path: Write | Type/Edit

Description: Positions the cursor on a specific page and line in the document.

Procedure:
1. Press F8 from the Type/Edit screen to display the Options Menu.

2. Select Other Options and press Enter.

3. From the Other Options Submenu select Go to Page/Line and press Enter.

4. Type the number of the page to which you would like to move, then press Enter.

5. Type the number of the line on the page to which you would like to move, then press Enter or F10 to move the cursor.

Notes: You may also execute this command by pressing Ctrl-F7 from the Type/Edit screen.

If you do not specify a line number, you will be placed on the first line of the specified page. If you do not enter a page number, but just a line number, you will be placed on the specified line of the document, counting from the first line of the first page.

Optionally, you may "place a bookmark" by pressing F5 to copy the current cursor location into the Goto box.

**Valid
Keystrokes:** F5—Copy current cursor location into the Goto box.

Hyphenate

Menu Path: Write I Type/Edit

Description: Inserts a soft hyphen at the cursor location. A soft hyphen will allow a word to remain whole if it will fit entirely on one line, or automatically break with a hyphen instead of wrapping it if it will not fit.

Procedure: 1. Press F8 from the Type/Edit screen to display the Options Menu.

2. Select Other Options and press Enter.

3. From the Other Options Submenu select Hyphenate and press Enter.

4. The character before the cursor will be enhanced to indicate the location of the soft hyphen. While the surrounding text is being edited, the word with the hyphen will automatically be split and rejoined as necessary.

Notes: You may also execute this command by pressing Alt-F6 from the Type/Edit screen.

Import a Document

Menu Path: Write I Utilities I Import a Document

Description: Imports documents from several other formats.

Procedure: 1. Select Import a Document from the Write Utilities Menu.

2. Select the document format from which to import. The following is a list of available formats and the versions supported:

   ASCII

   Special ASCII

   Macintosh ASCII

   DCA

   WordStar—Versions 3.3, 3.31, 3.45, 4.0, 5.0, 5.5

   WordPerfect—Versions 5.0, 5.1

   Microsoft Word—Versions 3.0, 3.1, 4.0, 5.0

   MultiMate—Versions 3.3, 3.6, 3.7, 4

   PFS: Write—Version C

   Professional Write—Versions 1.0, 2.0, 2.1

   PFS: First Choice—Versions 1.0, 2.0

3. Type the name of the file you want to import and press Enter.

4. Type a new name for the document in its Q&A format and press Enter.

See Also: *Export a Document*

Insert a Document _____

Menu Path: Write | Type/Edit

Description: Inserts a document into the currently loaded Q&A Write document at the cursor position.

Procedure: 1. Place the cursor at the position where you would like to insert the document.

2. Press F8 to display the Options Menu.

3. Select the Documents option to display the sub-menu.

4. Select the Insert a Document option from the sub-menu.

5. Type the name of the document to insert, and press Enter.

6. If the document is not recognized as a Q&A document, the Import Document Menu will appear. Select the appropriate format and press Enter.

7. The body of the document being inserted will appear at the cursor position.

See Also: *Get* for additional information on the Import Document Menu.

Lay Out Page

Menu Path: Write | Type/Edit

Description: Allows you to specify the page dimensions, set tabs, and edit the header and footer of the document. In addition, page breaks can be inserted and the Draw command can be accessed.

Procedure: 1. Press F8 from the Type/Edit screen to display the Options Menu.

2. Select Lay Out Page and press Enter. The Lay Out Page Submenu displays the following options:

Edit Header—Allows you to type information that will appear in the top margin on each page of the document.

Edit Footer—Allows you to type information that will appear in the bottom margin on each page of the document.

Define Page—Controls page dimensions, margin settings, and the printed text width. Also specifies on which page headers and footers begin and which page number to use on the first page that has a header or footer.

Set Tabs—Allows you to add or remove tab stops for the current document.

Newpage—Forces a page break at a specified location in the text.

Draw—Allows you to draw lines and boxes in the document.

See Also: *Edit Header and Footer*
                  Define Page in the General Chapter.
                  Set Tabs
                  Newpage
                  Draw

List Fields _____

Menu Path: Write | Type/Edit

Description: Displays a list of fields from a selected database for
                  insertion into the current document for merging pur-
                  poses.

Procedure: 1. Place the cursor at the location in the document
                     where you want to insert data from the database.

                  2. Press F8 from the Type/Edit screen to display the
                     Options Menu.

                  3. Select Other Options to display the submenu.

                  4. Select List Fields from the Other Options Sub-
                     menu.

                  5. If this is the first time you are inserting a merge
                     field, you will be prompted for a database name.
                     Type in the name of a Q&A database.

                  6. At the list of field names, select the field that you
                     want to insert in the document, and press Enter.
                     The merge field will appear between asterisks
                     (these do not print) in the document at the cursor
                     position.

Notes: You may also execute this command by pressing Alt-
                  F7 from the Type/Edit screen.

                  You may select the field from the list either by using
                  the up and down arrow keys to scroll through the
                  list, or by typing the first few letters of the field
                  name. As you type the letters appearing in the field
                  name, Q&A will highlight the field with matching
                  letters. Type until the desired field is highlighted.

See Also: *Mail Merge* for additional information on creating a
                  merge document.

_____ *List Files*

See *DOS File Facilities* in the Utilities Chapter.

_____ *Lowercase Block*

See *Block Operations*

_____ *Mail Merge*

Description: Allows selected records from a database to be sorted, and data from the fields to be placed at user-defined locations in a document. A document will print for each selected record.

Procedure: 1. Get the document in which to insert data or create the document as you follow the steps below. A document in which data is merged from a Q&A database is called a Mail Merge document. It will contain portions that are the same for every copy of the document to be printed, and portions that act as place holders for data to be inserted from the database.

2. Place the cursor at the location in the document where you want to insert data from the database.

3. Press Alt-F7 to insert a merge field. If this is the first time you are inserting a merge field, you will be prompted for a database name. Type in the name of a Q&A database.

4. At the list of field names, select the field that you want to insert in the document, and press Enter. The merge field will appear between asterisks (these do not print) in the document at the cursor position. You may apply simple formatting to a merge field (i.e., left, right justify, or trimming spaces) by inserting the appropriate code (L, R, T) within parentheses, after the field name but before the closing asterisk.

5. Repeat steps 2 through 4 for any additionally required fields.

6. When you have finished, save the document.

Notes: Field names do to not have to be inserted from the list of fields; they can be typed at the desired location as long as they appear between asterisks. If the asterisks are omitted, the field name will not be replaced by data, but will print as it appears in the document.

The list of field names may not coincide exactly with the fields on the form itself. This list is created from the names in the *Set Field Names* command to ensure that all fields have a unique name.

Avoid using field names in the mail merge document that correspond to Print Commands (*SS number* will try to print a spreadsheet called Number). If the situation occurs, use the *Set Field Names* command to assign to this field a different internal name for use in the field name lists. You may also enter a name that differs from the name in the Set Field Names command and then use the Identifier Spec to match the new name with a field.

Programming expressions may be used in merge documents to extract data from more than one database, or to create derived values for use in the document.

Examples: Here is an example of a mail merge letter, beginning with the address block:

```
*First Name* *Last Name*
*Address*
*City*, *State* *Zip*
Dear *First Name*,
```

You have been selected as a part of an elite group to attend our free seminar on buying real estate.

See Also: *Merge Field Formatting* for information on formatting the merged data.

Set Field Names in the File Chapter for additional information on modifying the internal field names used in creating the field name list, and in progamming expressions.

Print Commands for information on commands that will cause problems if used as field names.

Mailing Labels

Menu Path:	Write I Mailing Labels
Description:	Allows the creation, modification, or printing of mailing labels.
Procedure:	1. Select Mailing Labels from the Write Menu.

2. At the list of available label definitions, select one to modify or print, or type in the name of a new label definition to create. The name of the label definition can be up to 32 characters in length. In some cases it may be easier to copy an existing label to a new name, and then modify the copy.

3. The label will appear on the screen. A mailing label is nothing more than a single page Q&A Write document with a small page size. Mailing labels are usually used to merge information from a Q&A database, however mail merge fields are not required on a mailing label. Edit the label as you would any other Q&A Write document. All Type/ Edit keystrokes and commands are available. The Options Menu can be invoked with the F8 key as in Type/Edit, however, the Documents Option is not available.

4. To modify the label size, press Ctrl-F6 to display the Define Label screen. Set the following values:

   Width—The distance from the left edge of the label to the right edge of the label.

   Height—The distance from the top edge of the label to the top edge of the next label.

   Left Margin—The distance from the left edge of the label to the first possible character on each line of the label.

   Right Margin—The distance from the right edge of the label to the last possible character on each line of the label.

   Top Margin—The distance from the top edge of the label to the first line of the label.

   Bottom Margin—The distance from the bottom edge of the label to the last line of the label.

Characters Per Inch—The number of characters to print per inch across the page. The default value is 10.

Press F10 when you finish modifying the label dimensions.

5. Press Shift-F8 to save the label when you have finished editing, or F10 to save the label and display the Mailing Label Print Options.

6. To print the label, the Print Options need to be set. If you are not at the Mailing Label Print Options, press F2 from the label definition screen. Set the following options as required:

Number of Copies—Specify the number of copies to print. The limit is 32000. The default value is 1.

Print Offset—A whole number to align the print head with the left edge of the paper. Entering a positive value moves the head to the right, and a negative value moves the head to the left. The default value is 0.

Print To—Select the destination for the output, which is either an "installed printer" (PtrA, PtrB, PtrC, PtrD, PtrE), DISK, or SCREEN.

Page Preview—Preview the output instead of sending it to the selection in the Print To option. If you select YES the output will appear on your monitor in a graphics mode. If you select NO the output will be sent directly to the selection in the Print To option. The default value is NO.

Type of Paper Feed—Determines the source for the paper that is used for the output. Select MANUAL if you are hand feeding the labels, CONTINUOUS if you are using fanfold labels or a laser printer with a single bin, or BIN1, BIN2, or BIN3 when using a cut-sheet feeder or laser printer with multiple bins. The default value is CONTINUOUS.

Number of Labels Across—Specifies the number of labels to print on each row of labels. To print more than a single label per row, select a number from 1 to 8. The default value is 1 for new labels.

Space between Labels—Determines the space between columns of labels. The default value is 1 for new labels.

Lines per Label Sheet—Specifies the number of lines the printer can physically print on a page of labels. If you are using continuous pin fed labels as opposed to label sheets on a laser printer, then this value should be set to the number of lines in height of the label. The default value is 60 for new labels.

Blank Lines at Top—Specifies the number of lines at the top of the label sheet before the top of the first label on the page. This applies to label sheets printed on a laser printer; therefore, if you are using continuous pin fed labels, set this to 0. The default value is 0 for new labels.

Blank Lines at Bottom—Specifies the number of lines at the bottom of the label sheet below the bottom of the last label on the page. This applies to label sheets printed on a laser printer; therefore, if you are using continuous pin fed labels, set this to 0. The default value is 0 for new labels.

Printer Control Codes—Specify printer dependent codes for controlling special effects on your printer. These codes are sent to the printer before any data is sent.

Name of Merge File—Specifies the name of the database file to use for mail merging purposes. See the Mail Merge command for additional information. Press F10 to begin the printing process. If you have included mail merge fields, you may see the Retrieve, Sort, and Identifier Specs before actually printing.

Notes: Although the default values on the Define Label screen are in inches, the label dimensions and margin values can be entered in centimeters or characters. To specify these values in centimeters follow the number with the letters cm; for characters type in the value.

The higher the characters per inch setting (cpi) on the Define Label screen, the more characters will print across the label. If your printer does not support the selected cpi, the text will print in the next highest cpi available. This value will be overridden by fonts or other enhancements applied to text.

**Valid
Keystrokes:** F2—At the label editing screen or the Define Label screen, displays the Print Options screen

Ctrl-F6—At the label editing screen, displays the Define Label screen

Alt-F7—At the label editing screen, displays the List of Fields

F8—At the label editing screen, displays the Options Menu

Shift-F8—At the label editing screen, saves the label

F9—At the Print Options, returns to the label editing screen

F10—At the label editing screen, saves and displays the Print Options screen

See Also: *Type/Edit* for information on available editing keystrokes and commands.

Mail Merge for information on using merge fields on the label.

Merge Field Formatting for information on changing formatting attributes for the merged data on the label.

Install Printer in the Utilities Chapter for information on setting up your printers.

Page Preview in the General Chapter for information on previewing prior to printing.

Merge Field Formatting

Description: Allows data merged from a database in a mail merge document to be formatted (i.e., left or right justified, or with extra spaces trimmed) when the document is printed.

Procedure:

1. Place the cursor at the end of the merge field name to format.

2. Insert the desired formatting code between parentheses immediately following the merge field name. The following are available codes:

    T—if you have undesired tabs or returns in the data, use this code to remove the undesired tabs or returns from the data for this document.

    L—to line up merge field columns, use this code to left-justify data in the merge field between the asterisks.

    R—to line up merge field columns, use this code to right-justify data in the merge field between the asterisks.

Examples:

```
        Description                 Code

*Item1 Description(L)  *  *Item1 Code(R) *
*Item2 Description(L)  *  *Item2 Code(R) *
```

The L and R codes may be used in conjunction with spaces inserted after the merge field names to line up merge field columns.

See Also: *Mail Merge* for information on creating a merge document.

Move Block

See *Block Operations*

Move Block to File

See *Block Operations*

Newpage

Menu Path: Write | Type/Edit

Description: Forces a page break at a specified location in the text.

Procedure: 1. Position the cursor on the line of text that should begin on a new page.

2. Press F8 to display the Options Menu. Select Lay Out Page and press Enter.

3. From the Lay Out Page Submenu select Newpage and press Enter.

Notes: To remove a Newpage from a document, delete the Newpage symbol (⏎) that appears at the location where the Newpage was entered.

Options Menu _____

Description: Accesses editing options for laying out the page, aligning text, performing block operations, working with documents, and many others.

Procedure: 1. Press F8 from the Type/Edit screen to display the Options Menu.

2. The Options Menu consists of two menus, a main menu and a changing submenu. The main menu contains the following selections:

Lay Out Page—Allows you to specify the page dimensions, set tabs, and edit the header and footer of the document. In addition, hard page breaks can be inserted and the Draw command can be accessed.

Documents—Displays a list of the last 12 documents that were edited. You may select one of those documents, get a new one, or insert a document into the current one.

Align Text—Allows you to justify text to the right or left as well as center text. You can select to display single, double, or triple line spacing, and you can set temporary margins.

Block Operations—Allows you to copy, move, delete, enhance, or print a block of text. Also, you can change a block to all uppercase letters, all lowercase, or title capitalization.

Print Commands—Displays a list of available print commands and inserts them into the document with the necessary parameters. Some of the commands insert a graph or spreadsheet, or stamp the date or time at print time.

Other Options—Accesses the spell checker or the-saurus. Gets document statistics or performs column calculations. Accesses Search and Re-place as well as many others options.

See Also: *Lay Out Page*
Documents
Align Text
Block Operations
Print Commands
Other Options
Type/Edit to create new documents.

Other Options

Menu Path: Write | Type/Edit

Description: Accesses the spell checker or thesaurus. Gets document statistics or performs column calculations. Accesses Search and Replace as well as many other options.

Procedure: 1. Press F8 from the Type/Edit screen to display the Options Menu.

2. Select Other Options and press Enter. The Other Options Submenu displays the following options:

Spellcheck—Spellchecks the document from the current location to the end of the document.

Spellcheck Word—Spellchecks the current word.

Thesaurus—Checks the thesaurus for synonyms for the current word.

Statistics—Displays a window of document statistics.

Hyphenate—Inserts a soft hyphen at the cursor location.

Search & Replace—Performs a search and optional replace in the document.

Restore—Restores the most recently deleted or copied text.

Go to Page/Line—Positions the cursor on a specific line of a specific page in the document.

List Fields—Displays a list of fields from a Q&A database for insertion into a mail merge document.

Save—Saves the document to disk.

Save as ASCII—Saves the document to disk in an ASCII format.

Assign Fonts—Accesses the Font Assignments screen to select fonts from a Q&A font file.

Calculate—Performs column or row mathematics.

See Also: *Spellcheck*

Thesaurus

Statistics

Hyphenate

Search & Replace

Restore

Go to Page/Line

List Fields

Save

Save as ASCII

Font Assignments in the General Chapter.

Calculate

Print _____

Menu Path: Write I Print

Description: Displays the Print Options screen for modification, and prints the currently loaded document.

Procedure: 1. Select Print from the Write Menu.

2. At the Print Options screen, set the options to your preference. Optionally, press Ctrl-F6 to display the Define Page screen.

3. Press F10 to print.

Notes: The document currently loaded for editing will be printed. If no document is loaded, Q&A will not execute this command.

Valid
Keystrokes: Ctrl-F6—At the Print Options screen to display the
Define Page screen

F9—At the Print Options screen to return to the Write
Menu

See Also: *Print Options* and *Define Page* in the General
Chapter.

Get for information on loading a document.

_____ *Print Block*

See *Block Operations*

_____ *Print Commands*

Menu Path: Write | Type/Edit

Description: Displays a list of available print commands and inserts them into the document with the necessary parameters. Some of the commands insert a graph or
spreadsheet, or stamp the date or time. The effects of
these commands will be viewed only when the document is printed.

Procedure: 1. Press F8 from the Type/Edit screen to display the
Options Menu.

2. Select Print Commands and press Enter. Select the
desired Print Command from the Print Commands
Submenu:

   Date—Stamps the current date into the document
   using the syntax *@DATE(n)* with "n" as a
   number from 1 to 20 referring to the desired
   date format from those found in *Format Values*
   in the File Chapter.

   Filename—Stamps the filename into the document
   using the syntax *FILENAME*.

   Graph—Inserts a Lotus 1-2-3 or Symphony .PIC
   file, or a PFS: Graph picture file into the document using the syntax *GRAPH filename, s/d/
   q, font1, font2, width, height, rotation*. You
   may substitute G for the word GRAPH.

Filename—This is the name of the graphics file.

S/D/Q—This refers to single, double, or quadruple density. S is the default.

The remaining parameters are for use only with Lotus or Symphony .PIC files:

Font1—This optional parameter is the filename of a Lotus font file. BLOCK1.FNT is the default.

Font2—This optional parameter is the filename of a Lotus font file. The default is BLOCK1.FNT or whatever was specified as Font1.

Width—This optional parameter is a decimal number representing the width in inches. The default is 6.5.

Height—This optional parameter is a decimal number representing the height in inches. The default is 4.7.

Rotation—This optional parameter is a number representing the number of degrees to rotate the graph counterclockwise. The only valid choices are 0, 90, 180, and 270. The default is 0.

Join—Inserts the text of a document into the body of the current document, using the margins, headers, and footers of the current document. The syntax is *JOIN filename* where filename is the name of the file to join. You may substitute J for the word JOIN.

Justify—Turns justification on or off using the syntax *JUSTIFY yes/no*. Replace yes/no with YES if the following text should be justified, or NO if the following text should be unjustified. You may substitute JY for the word JUSTIFY and Y or N for the words YES and NO.

Linespacing—Allows line spacing to be changed from 1 to 9 lines between each printed line using the syntax *LINESPACING n* with "n" being the number of lines to space. You may substitute LS for the word LINESPACING.

Postfile—Embeds a PostScript program file in the document using the syntax *POSTFILE filename* where filename is the name of the PostScript program file. You may substitute PF for the word POSTFILE.

Postscript—Sends a single PostScript command to your PostScript printer using the syntax *POSTSCRIPT PostScript commands* where PostScript commands are the commands to be sent to the printer. You may substitute PS for the word POSTSCRIPT.

Printer—Sends printer control codes to your non-PostScript printer using the syntax *PRINTER print codes* where printer codes are the ASCII decimal equivalents of the codes to send to the printer. You may substitute P for the word PRINTER.

Program—Embeds a mail merge programming statement into your document using the syntax *PROGRAM {statements}*. See *Programming Chapter* to replace statements with valid mail merge programming statements. You may substitute PG for the word PROGRAM.

Queue—Begins printing the specified document at the current location. The queued document retains its own headers, footers, and pagination. Page characteristics and font assignments are controlled by the master document. Use the syntax *QUEUE filename* with filename being the file you want to queue. You may substitute Q for the word QUEUE.

QueueP—This functions like Queue, except the pagination of the queued document is consistent with the document in which it is placed. Use the syntax *QUEUEP filename* with filename being the file you want to queue. You may substitute QP for the word QUEUEP.

Spreadsheet—Embeds a Lotus 1-2-3 Spreadsheet (or portion thereof) into the current document using the syntax *SPREADSHEET filename, range* where filename is the name of the spreadsheet and range is the name of the range of cells in the spreadsheet, or the upper-left and lower-right cell coordinates of a range. You may substitute SS for the word SPREAD-SHEET.

Stop—Stops printing until Enter is pressed using the syntax *STOP*. You may substitute S for the word STOP.

Time—Stamps the current time into the document using the syntax *@TIME(n)* with "n" as a number from 1 to 3 referring to the desired time format from the following list:

1—4:55 pm

2—16:55

3—16.55

Print Options, Write _____

See *Print Options* in the General Chapter.

Recover a Document _____

Menu Path:	Write I Utilities I Recover a Document
Description:	Recovers the text of a damaged document.
Procedure:	1. Select Recover a Document from the Write Utilities Menu.
	2. Type the name of the document to recover.
	3. Read and follow the instructions on the warning screen.
	4. Press F10 to recover the document.
Notes:	Make a backup copy of the document before trying to Recover a Document.

The recovered document will not contain the Define Page, headers, footers, font assignments, tab settings, or Print Options from the original document.

If any part of the enhancements in the document were not recoverable, the character ε will appear in its place. You may search for this character and replace it with the correct information.

Rename a Document

See *DOS File Facilities* in the Utilities Chapter.

Restore

Menu Path:	Write I Type/Edit
Description:	Restores the text from the clipboard. The text in the clipboard is that which was involved in the most recent Copy, Move, or Delete operation.
Procedure:	1. Place the cursor at the location to restore the text. Press F8 from the Type/Edit screen to display the Options Menu.
	2. Select Other Options and press Enter.
	3. From the Other Options Submenu select Restore and press Enter.
Notes:	The clipboard contents are replaced each time one of the following operations is used:

> **Delete**—This includes all forms of Delete (e.g., Delete Word, Delete Line, Delete Block, etc.) except deleting one letter at a time with the Delete key.
>
> **Move Block**
>
> **Copy Block**

The clipboard is not cleared when you get another document. This allows text from one document to be moved to another document without retyping it.

You may also execute this command by pressing Shift-F7 from the Type/Edit screen.

See Also:	*Block Operations*

Save

Menu Path:	Write I Save
Description:	Saves the currently loaded document.

Procedure:	1. Press F8 from the Type/Edit screen to display the Options Menu.
	2. Select Other Options to display the submenu.
	3. Select Save.
	4. Type in the name to give the document, and press Enter.
Notes:	You may also execute this command by pressing Shift-F8 from the Type/Edit screen, or selecting the Save option from the Write Menu.
See Also:	*Save as ASCII* for information on saving the document in an ASCII format.

Save as ASCII _____

Menu Path:	Write I Type/Edit
Description:	Saves the currently loaded document as an ASCII file. Saving a file in an ASCII format will not retain page formatting, fonting, headers, footers, tab settings, or print options.
Procedure:	1. Press F8 from the Type/Edit screen to display the Options Menu.
	2. Select Other Options to display the submenu.
	3. Select Save as ASCII.
	4. Type in the name to give the ASCII file and press Enter.
Notes:	You may also execute this command by pressing Ctrl-F8 at the Type/Edit screen.
See Also:	*Save* for information on saving a document in the default Q&A Write format.

Search & Replace _____

Menu Path:	Write I Type/Edit
Description:	Searches the document for matching text and can replace it with other text.

Procedure:

1. Press F8 from the Type/Edit screen to display the Options Menu.

2. Select Other Options and press Enter.

3. From the Other Options Submenu select Search & Replace and press Enter.

4. Enter or choose values for the following:

   Search for—This is the text for which to search. It can be one word, or several words.

   Replace with—This is the text to replace the text that was searched for. This may be left blank.

   Method—This specifies the search method. The following are the available options:

   Manual—This pauses each time a match is found. After each match you may press F7 to find the next match, and if you specified a Replace string, press F10 to replace and continue, or press Esc to cancel.

   Automatic—All matches are automatically replaced without prompting for confirmation.

   Fast Automatic—This option is similar to Automatic except that the screen is not updated each time a match is found. This has a positive impact on performance for large Search & Replace operations.

5. Optionally, you may press PgDn and set the Advanced Options:

   Type—This specifies how to interpret the search string. There are three options:

   Whole Words—This indicates that the search string is made up of complete words. With this type set, a search string of "cat" will not find "scatter."

   Text—This setting allows the search string to be found anywhere, even within words. For example, the search string "how" will find both "how," and "shower."

   Pattern—This allows a search for a pattern, such as two letters followed by three num-

bers, which would be designated as
"AA999."

Case—This setting indicates whether or not to
check the case of the search string:

Insensitive—This setting allows matches to be
capitalized differently from the search string.
A case-insensitive search for "bat" will find
both "bat" and "Bat."

Sensitive—This setting forces matches to be
capitalized exactly like the search string. A
case-sensitive search for "now" will not find
"NOW."

Range—This controls where in the document the
search will take place. The available settings
are:

All—This searches the entire document. It
starts from the current cursor location and
searches to the end of the document, then
restarts the search from the top of the document down to the original starting point.

To End—This searches from the current cursor
location to the end of the document.

To Beginning—This searches backwards from
the current cursor location to the beginning
of the document.

Search Joins—This setting indicates whether the
search operation should continue across documents that are connected to the current document by the Print Commands: Join, Queue, and
QueueP. YES will conduct the search across the
connected documents. NO will restrict the
search to the current document.

6. Press F10 to begin the search operation.

7. If you selected Manual for the Method option, you
will be prompted after each match is found. You
may press F7 to skip this match and search for the
next one, or, if you specified a replace string, press
F10 to replace this match and then search for the
next one, or press Escape to cancel the search.

Notes: You may also execute this command by pressing F7 from the Type/Edit screen.

You may enter search strings with wildcard characters in addition to literal text.

Table 4.1 gives the available wildcard characters:

Table 4.1. Wildcard Characters

Char	Meaning	Example
?	Represents a single character.	?at—Finds mat, bat and sat, but not flat.
..	Represents any number of alphanumeric characters.	r..d—Finds rigid, rapid, and road, but not ready, nor deer.
\	Search for the literal meaning of the next character.	\?—Finds a single question mark. \\—Finds a single backslash character. \ \—Finds three consecutive space characters.
@	Begins a Special Search Function.	@CR—Finds all carriage returns.

You may search for many things that cannot be represented in the search string (e.g., a tab character). These characters and attributes can be represented with the Special Search Functions shown in Table 4.2:

Table 4.2. Special Search Functions

Function	Meaning
Special Characters and Attributes	
@CR	Finds a single carriage return.
@TB	Finds a single tab character.
@NP	Finds a Newpage symbol.
@CT	Finds centered text.
Enhancements and Fonts	
@RG	Finds regular text (no enhancements).
@BD	Finds bold face text.
@UL	Finds underlined text.
@IT	Finds italicized text.
@SP	Finds superscript text.
@SB	Finds subscript text.
@XO	Finds text with the strikeout enhancement.
@Fn	Finds font "n" when n is from 1 to 8.

To search for patterns of characters, you must specify Pattern for the Type option. Then you may enter the desired pattern using the following characters (Table 4.3):

Table 4.3.   Pattern Search Wildcards

Char	Meaning
9	Any single numeric digit (0–9).
a or A	Any single alphabetic character (A–Z).
?	Any single alphanumeric character (0–9 or A–Z).
~	Any single nonalphanumeric character (e.g., $).

In a pattern search, all nonwildcard characters in the search string are treated literally.

Examples:

Table 4.4.   Search and Replace Samples

Search String	Description
Michelle	A simple text search that finds the word Michelle.
@BDwatch	Search for enhanced text. This finds all boldfaced watches.
AA999	As a pattern search, this would find all occurrences of two letters followed by three numbers.
99\999	As a pattern search, this finds all five numeral strings with a 9 in the third position.

Valid Keystrokes: PgDn—Display the Advanced Options

F7—During manual search to continue without replacement

F10 —During manual search to replace and then continue

Set Editing Options

Menu Path: Write I Utilities I Set Global Options I Set Editing Options

Description: Modifies options in effect during editing of all documents.

Procedure: 1. Select Set Editing Options from the Global Options Menu.

2. Modify the following editing options:

Default Editing Mode—Select INSERT if you want new text entered to be inserted between existing text, or OVERTYPE to type over existing text. This value may be toggled while editing a document by pressing the Insert key. The default is OVERTYPE.

Default Export Type—Determines how Ctrl-F8 (Save as ASCII) saves ASCII documents. Select ASCII with CR to place a carriage return at the end of each line, or ASCII without CR to save each line without a carriage return. The default is ASCII with CR.

Automatic Backups—Select YES to create a backup copy of your document each time you load it for editing. The backup file is saved with the same document name with a .BAK extension. The default is NO.

Use Real Tab Characters—Uses real tabs when the Tab key is pressed instead of spaces. Allows the placement of position specific information for the proper alignment of text. This is useful for tabbed columns when printing with a proportional spaced font. The default is NO.

Show Tabs On Screen—Select YES to display an arrow (▶) representing real tab characters in a document. The default is NO.

Show Returns On Screen—Select YES to display hard returns (not those created by word wrapping) with a paragraph marker (¶).

Decimal Convention—Determines the character with which decimal tabs align, and how column/row math interprets numbers. Select AMERICAN to use a period, or EUROPEAN to use a comma as the decimal.

Show Margins On Screen—Determines whether or not Q&A displays the margins on screen. Selecting NO will not display the margins, and will therefore allow more room on the screen for displaying text. The default is YES.

Show Ghost Cursor—Determines whether or not
the ghost cursor is displayed or not. The ghost
cursor is the rectangular block on the ruler line
that tracks the cursor position. The default is
YES.

Default Import Type—Sets the format used to import non-Q&A Write documents when using
the Get Document command to load a document. If the option is set to NONE, the Import
Document Menu is automatically displayed
when non-Q&A Write documents are encountered. The default is NONE.

Default Tab Settings—Sets the columns to use for
default tab stops. The default tab settings are at
columns 5, 15, 25, and 35.

Spacing Between Columns—Sets the space between columns for documents printed with
more than a single column. To enter a value in
centimeters, follow the number with the letters
cm. To enter a value in characters, enter the
number representing the column. The default
value is .25".

See Also: *Get* for information on the Import Document Menu.

Print Options in the General Chapter for information on printing documents with more than one column.

Set Tabs for information on setting tabs for a single
document.

Set Global Options _____

Menu Path: Write I Utilities I Set Global Options

Description: Allows modification of editing options and global
print, page, and import options.

Procedure: 1. Select Set Global Options from the Write Utilities
Menu.

2. At the Global Options Menu select one of the following options:

Set Editing Options—Modifies options in effect
during editing of a document.

  Change Print Defaults—Modifies Print Options
   for all new documents.

  Change Page Defaults—Modifies Define Page options for all new documents.

  Change Import Defaults—Modifies Define Page
   options for documents imported via the Get
   Document command.

See Also: *Set Editing Options*

      Change Print Defaults

      Define Page and *Print Options* in the General Chap-
      ter.

      Change Page Defaults

      Change Import Defaults

Set Tabs

Menu Path: Write | Type/Edit

Description: Allows you to add or remove tab stops for the cur-
      rent document.

Procedure: 1. Press F8 from the Type/Edit screen to display the
       Options Menu.

      2. Select Lay Out Page and press Enter.

      3. From the Lay Out Page Submenu select Set Tabs
       and press Enter.

      4. Move the cursor to the right or left along the ruler
       line at the bottom of the page. Type one of the
       following codes at each location to place a tab
       stop:

       T—This specifies a regular tab stop. Tab to this
        stop and the following text will be aligned with
        other text on this tab stop.

       D—This specifies a decimal tab stop. Numbers
        typed at this tab stop will be aligned at their
        decimal points.

      5. To clear a tab stop, position the cursor under it
       and press the spacebar.

      6. Press F10 when finished.

Notes: The numbers along the ruler line are inch markers.

**Valid
Keystrokes:**   Tab—Move the cursor to the next tab stop

Shift-Tab—Move the cursor to the previous tab stop

Set Temporary Margins _____

Menu Path: Write | Type/Edit

Description: Allows margins to be set for blocks of text that require margins that are different from the rest of the document, or clears previously set temporary margins.

Procedure: 1. Place the cursor on the line at which you would like to set the temporary margin, or clear previously set temporary margins. If you are setting a temporary margin, place the cursor at the location to set the margin.

2. Press F8 from the Type/Edit screen to display the Options Menu.

3. Select Align Text to display the submenu.

4. Select the Temp Margins option to display the Temporary Margins Menu.

5. To set a left margin, select Left. To set a right margin, select Right. To clear all temporary margins, select Clear.

Notes: You may also execute this command by pressing F6 from the Type/Edit screen.

Temporary margins act like regular document margins. Setting a left margin will place the cursor at the set position for subsequent lines if a carriage return is entered, or if word wrapping occurs. Setting a right margin will cause word wrap at the set position. Text can be entered to the left of a temporary left margin by using the arrow keys to place the cursor at the desired location. The same does not apply for temporary right margins. If text is entered to the right of the margin, it will be forced to the next line.

_____ *Spellcheck*

Menu Path:	Write I Type/Edit
Description:	Checks the spelling of the document, displays a list of possible corrections, and allows unknown words to be stored in a personal dictionary.
Procedure:	1. Press F8 from the Type/Edit screen to display the Options Menu.

2. Select Other Options and press Enter.

3. From the Other Options Submenu select Spellcheck and press Enter.

4. The spelling will be checked from the cursor location to the end of the document. Whenever a misspelled word is encountered, it is highlighted, and a menu of the following options will appear:

   List Possible Spellings—This option will display a list of up to nine words that might be the correct spelling of the highlighted word. You may then either select a word from the list or press ESC to return to the menu of choices. If there are no possible spellings for the highlighted word, then a box will appear asking you to press Enter to continue.

   Ignore Word & Continue—This option will bypass this word and all other occurrences of it in the document. The spellcheck will continue after selecting this option.

   Add to Dictionary & Continue—This option will add the highlighted word to the user's personal dictionary. The personal dictionary is a way to store words that are not in Q&A's main dictionary, but you want Q&A to bypass whenever they appear in a document. The spellcheck will continue after selecting this option.

   Add to Dictionary & Stop—This option will add the highlighted word to the user's personal dictionary. The spellcheck will stop after selecting this option.

   Edit Word & Recheck—This option allows the word to be edited and then rechecked. The highlighted word is placed into a window for editing; make the necessary changes and then press Enter to recheck the spelling.

5. If a word is repeated twice in a row, the second occurrence will be highlighted and a message will appear asking you to press F3 to delete the word, or press Enter to continue.

Notes: You may also execute this command by pressing Shift-F1 from the Type/Edit screen.

To Check the spelling of a single word, you may select Spellcheck Word from the Other Options Menu, or press Ctrl-F1 from the Type/Edit screen.

The personal dictionary is stored as an alphabetized ASCII file with one word on each line. The filename is QAPERS.DCT. It may be edited by loading it as an ASCII document. If you edit it make sure all of the words are in alphabetical order, and it is saved as ASCII.

See Also: *Get* to get the QAPERS.DCT file for editing.

Statistics _____

Menu Path: Write I Type/Edit

Description: Displays the total number of words, lines, and paragraphs in the current document.

Procedure: 1. Press F8 from the Type/Edit screen to display the Options Menu.

2. Select Other Options and press Enter.

3. From the Other Options Submenu select Document Statistics and press Enter.

4. The document statistics box displays the number of words, lines, and paragraphs for each of three areas of the document: Up to the cursor, from the cursor to the end of the document, and the entire document.

Notes: You may also execute this command by pressing Ctrl-F3 from the Type/Edit screen.

_____ *Thesaurus*

Menu Path: Write I Type/Edit

Description: Checks the built-in thesaurus for synonyms of the word at the cursor.

Procedure: 1. Place the cursor on the word to check in the thesaurus, and press F8 from the Type/Edit screen to display the Options Menu.

2. Select Other Options and press Enter.

3. From the Other Options Submenu select Thesaurus and press Enter. A list of synonyms will appear for the highlighted word. If the word could be used as different parts of speech, the list will be grouped by the parts of speech.

4. Use the arrow keys to select one of the synonyms. Optionally, you may press Alt-F1 to view a list of synonyms for that word, or continue to the next step. If you press Alt-F1 to display more lists of synonyms, you may at any time press F9 to return to a previous list.

5. Press F10 to replace the highlighted word with the word at the cursor.

Notes: You may also execute this command by pressing Alt-F1 from the Type/Edit screen.

**Valid
Keystrokes:**   Alt-F1—Lookup another word

F9—Return to previous list

Shift-F9—Move to the next list after using F9

F10—Replace highlighted word with word at cursor

_____ *Title Block*

See *Block Operations*

_____ *Type/Edit*

Menu Path: Write I Type/Edit

Description: Allows editing of a new or existing Q&A Write document.

Procedure: 1. Select Type/Edit from the Write Menu to create a new document, or Get an existing document. The Type/Edit screen contains the following important items:

The Cursor—This is the blinking line or block on screen that indicates the current position where text will be placed if you type. If the cursor is a block you are in "Insert" mode, otherwise you are in "Overtype" mode. In Insert mode any text you type will be inserted at the cursor position pushing any existing text after the cursor to the right. In Overtype mode any text you type will be placed at the cursor position overtyping any text under the cursor.

Ruler Line—This is the line at the bottom of the editing area that spans the width of the document. In addition to the inch marks, the ruler line displays the current margins ([and]), any temporary margins in effect (< and >), tab stops (T or D), the ghost cursor, and the line spacing in effect (s—single, d—double, t—triple).

Name of the Document—The name of the document being currently edited appears on the line below the ruler line, to the far left or "Working Copy" if the document has just been created and not saved.

Memory Usage Indicator—The percent of memory used by the document being currently edited appears on the line below the ruler line, to the right, before the percent (%) sign.

Current Column Indicator—This is the column where the cursor is currently found. It appears on the line below the ruler line, after the memory usage indicator.

Current Line Indicator—This is the current line the cursor is on. It appears on the line below the ruler line, after the keyword "Line."

Current Page Information—The current page being edited, and the total number of pages in the document, appear on the line below the ruler line, on the far right.

State Indicators—These represent the current state of the Num Lock, Caps Lock, and Insert/Overtype mode; they appear on the line below the ruler line. If the Num Lock state is active (i.e., pressing keys on the numeric keypad produces numbers on screen) the letters "Num" will appear. If the Caps Lock state is active (i.e., all alphabetic keys produce uppercase letters on screen) the letters "Caps" will appear. If the Insert mode is active, the letters "Ins" will appear.

Font and Enhancement Indicators—These represent the fonts and enhancements of the character under the cursor; they appear on the line below the ruler line. The list in Table 4.5 contains the different font and enhancement abbreviations that appear:

Table 4.5. Font and Enhancement Abbreviations

Abbreviation	Description
Bold	Character is boldfaced.
Ital	Character is italicized.
Undl	Character is underlined.
Supr	Character is superscripted.
Subs	Character is subscripted.
Sout	Character is striked out.
Font1–8	Character is fonted with Font 1–8 unassigned.
other	Character is fonted with Font 1–8 assigned.

2. Begin typing text. When you come to the right margin, if you continue typing Q&A will automatically place the word (if necessary) and the cursor on the next line. This is called word wrap.

You may move the cursor around a document with the arrow and keypad keys, or with the mouse. To use the cursor and the keypad keys use the keystrokes shown in Table 4.6:

Table 4.6. Document Navigation

Keystroke	Action
Home	Move up in the document:
	—first time pressed, moves to the first character on the current line
	—second time pressed, moves to the top of the screen
	—third time pressed, moves to the top of the current page
	—fourth time pressed, moves to the beginning of the document
Ctrl-Home	Moves to the beginning of the document
End	Move down in the document:
	—first time pressed, moves to the last character on the current line
	—second time pressed, moves to the bottom of the screen
	—third time pressed, moves to the bottom of the current page
	—fourth time pressed, moves to the end of the document
Ctrl-End	Moves to the end of the document
Up Arrow	Moves up one line
Down Arrow	Moves down one line
Right Arrow	Move to the next character
Left Arrow	Moves to the previous character
Ctrl-Left Arrow	Moves to the first character of the previous word
Ctrl-Right Arrow	Moves to the first character of the next word
PgUp	Moves to the previous screen
Ctrl-PgUp	Moves to the first character of the previous page
PgDn	Moves to the next screen
Ctrl-PgDn	Moves to the first character of the next page
F9	Scrolls the screen up one line
Shift-F9	Scrolls the screen down one line

To access available editing options, press F8 to display the Options Menu.

3. To save the document press Shift-F8, and type in the name under which to save it.

Notes: Table 4.7 lists the different ways to delete text while editing a document:

Table 4.7. Deleting in a Document

To Delete	Action
Character	Position the cursor under the character to delete, and press the Delete key, or position the cursor immediately to the right of the character to delete, and press the Backspace key.
Word	Position the cursor under the first letter of the word to delete and press F4 (the space after the word will be deleted). If the cursor is not under the first character the part of the word from the cursor to the end of the word will be deleted (the space will not be deleted).
Line	Place the cursor on the line to delete, and press Shift-F4. To delete from the cursor to the end of the line, press Ctrl-F4.
Block	Place the cursor on the first character of the block to delete, and press F3. Use the arrow keys to highlight the block of text to delete, and press F10.

The most recently deleted text can be restored, by pressing Shift-F7.

Valid Keystrokes:

Alt-F1—Activate the thesaurus

Ctrl-F1—Check spelling of word

Shift-F1—Check spelling of the document

F2—Display Print Options

Ctrl-F2—Print text block

F3—Delete text block

Alt-F3—Display document statistics

F4—Delete word

Ctrl-F4—Delete to end of the current line

Shift-F4—Delete the current line

F5—Copy text block

Alt-F5—Move text block to file

Ctrl-F5—Copy text block to file

Shift-F5—Move text block

F6—Set temporary margins

Alt-F6—Set soft hyphen

Ctrl-F6—Display Define Page screen

Shift-F6—Enhance text block

F7— Search and Replace

Alt-F7—Display list of fields from merge database

Ctrl-F7—Go to page/line

Shift-F7—Restore most recently deleted text

F8—Display the Options Menu

Ctrl-F8—Save the document in an ASCII format

Shift-F8—Save the document

F9—Scroll screen up one line

Alt-F9—Calculate numbers

Ctrl-F9—Display the Font Assignments screen

Shift-F9—Scroll screen down one line

See Also: *Align Text* for information on formatting text.

Block Operations for information on manipulating blocks.

Other Options for information including Spellcheck, Thesaurus, and Calculate.

Statistics for information on displaying the number of words, paragraphs, and lines in a document.

Documents for information on loading the 12 most recently loaded documents.

Draw for information on drawing boxes in a document.

Edit Header and Footer for information on creating headers and footers in a document.

Get for information on loading a document.

Go to Page/Line for information on moving the cursor to the specified page, and line.

Hyphenate for information on hyphenating a word.

Insert a Document for information on inserting a document into the currently loaded document.

List Fields for information on listing fields in the database with which to create a merge document.

Mail Merge for information on creating a merge document.

Newpage for information on inserting a page break in a document.

Options Menu for information on available editing options.

Print Commands for information on inserting special commands to execute at printing time.

Print for information on printing a document.

Save for information on saving a document.

Search & Replace for information on searching and replacing text in a document.

Set Tabs for information on setting tabs in a document.

Set Temporary Margins for information on setting temporary margins.

Define Page and *Print Options* in the General Chapter.

Utilities

Menu Path: Write | Utilities

Description: Displays the Write Utilities Menu. The Write Utilities Menu allows you to set global options, import, export, recover documents, and perform DOS functions.

Procedure: 1. Select Utilities from the Write Menu.

2. The Write Utilities Menu displays the following choices:

Set Global Options—Allows you to set a default Define Page, Print Options, and Import Define Page screen. Also allows the setting of global editing options.

Import a Document—Allows documents to be imported from several other document formats.

Export a Document—Allows documents to be exported to several other document formats.

Recover a Document—Recovers the text of damaged documents.

DOS Facilities—Allows files to be listed, renamed, deleted, and copied.

See Also: *Set Global Options*
                     Import a Document
                     Export a Document
                     Recover a Document
                     DOS File Facilities in the General Chapter

5

Assistant

Q&A's Intelligent Assistant offers an alternate way of accessing information from a database. All information is accessed via English-like requests. These requests can be entered into the IA's Ask Box, or through the use of the Query Guide. The Query Guide helps in building requests for processing.

After teaching the Assistant and Query Guide about a database, questions can be asked to produce or run columnar and cross tab reports, or view, edit, and delete records.

Advanced Lessons

Menu Path: Assistant I Teach Me About Your Database I Advanced Lessons

Description: Teaches the Assistant adjectives, verbs, and units of measure that are specific to the database, and also which fields contain people's names.

Procedure: 1. Select Advanced Lessons from the Basic Lessons Menu.

2. The Advanced Lessons Menu displays the following options:

What Fields Contain People's Names—Specifies which fields in the database contain people's names.

Units of Measure—Teaches the Assistant which unit of measure (e.g., inches, pounds, miles) you will use with each numeric field.

Advanced Vocabulary: Adjectives—Teaches the Assistant adjectives describing high (e.g., heavy, old) and low values (e.g., light, young) for each numeric field.

> **Advanced Vocabulary: Verbs**—Teaches the Assistant verbs associated with fields that will be used to simplify requests.
>
> **Exit Lessons**—Exits the Advanced Lessons Menu.

See Also: *What Fields Contain People's Names*
            Units of Measure
            Advanced Vocabulary: Adjectives
            Advanced Vocabulary: Verbs

Advanced Vocabulary: Adjectives _____

Menu Path: Assistant I Teach Me About Your Database I Advanced Lessons I Advanced Vocabulary: Adjectives

Description: Teaches the Assistant adjectives describing high values and low values for each numeric and money field.

Procedure: 1. Select Advanced Vocabulary: Adjectives from the Advanced Lessons Menu.

2. If the database has no number or money fields, you will not be able to proceed because Adjectives can be defined only for numeric or monetary fields. See *Format Values* in the File Chapter to change your field's information type.

3. Use F6 and F8 to select the previous or next number or money field for which you want to define an adjective.

4. Type adjectives that describe high and/or low values into the selected field. Repeat steps 3 and 4 until finished (see Table 5.1 for examples).

5. Press F10 to continue.

Examples:

Table 5.1.   Sample Adjectives

Data	High Adjectives	Low Adjectives
Height	tall, big, high	short, small, low
Age	old, ancient, senior	young, new, junior
Weight	heavy, fat	light, skinny
Length	long	quick

...umber or money field

...er or money field

... File Chapter to change a field's

...anced Vocabulary: Verbs

...About Your Database | Ad-
...anced Vocabulary: Verbs

...verbs, associated with fields,
...sk simpler requests. Verbs can
...tionships between the data and
...IS $10000 implies that the sal-

Procedure:	1. Select Advanced Vocabulary: Verbs from the Advanced Lessons Menu.
	2. Use F6 and F8 to select the previous or next field for which you want to define a verb.
	3. Type one or more verbs into the box for the selected field. Each verb must be associated with only one field. The verbs entered here cannot be used as field names or alternate field names. Repeat steps 2 and 3 until finished.
	4. Press F10 to continue.
Notes:	If you are having difficulty determining which verbs to use with which fields, try substituting the field name into the phrase, ''has a _____ of.'' This can often help you focus on a good verb.

Examples:	Phrase	Implies Verb
	has a SALARY of	EARN
	has an ADDRESS of	LIVE

Valid Keystrokes:	F6—Select previous field
	F8—Select field
See Also:	*Alternate Field Names* to set or change a field's alternate names.

Alternate Field Names _____

Menu Path: Assistant | Teach Me About Your Database | Alternate Field Names

Description: Teaches the Assistant different names for your fields that can be used when creating requests.

Procedure: 1. Select Alternate Field Names from the Basic Lessons Menu.

2. Press F6 and F8 to select the previous or next field for which you want to teach Alternate Field Names.

3. Type up to ten synonyms for the selected field. The first name is already entered, and cannot be edited because it is set through the *Set Field Names* command in the File Chapter. Repeat steps 2 and 3 until finished.

4. Press F10 to continue.

Notes: Every alternate field name must be unique throughout the whole database.

Example: A Company field may have the alternate field names: Company, Company Name, Workplace, and Business.

See Also: *Set Field Names* in the File Chapter to edit the first alternate field name.

Ask Me To Do Something _____

Menu Path: Assistant | Ask Me To Do Something

Description: Allows English-like phrases to be entered for processing by the Intelligent Assistant. Requests to retrieve information, add information, modify information, or perform calculations can all be asked.

Procedure: 1. Select Ask Me To Do Something from the Assistant Menu.

2. At the IA Request screen, type in the request, and press Enter when finished.

3. Once the request has been fully understood, the Assistant will rephrase the request and ask you for verification. If the IA does not understand the re-

quest, or has problems with a particular word, the problem area will be highlighted and the IA will ask for clarification. If the rephrase is what you requested, answer YES to continue, otherwise answer NO.

4. If your request required the creation of a report, you may scroll through the report using the arrow, Pgup, and Pgdn keys. If your request required viewing, editing, or adding a record, all keystrokes and commands from either Search/Update (for viewing and editing) or Add Data (for adding) can be used. To print either a report or record, press the F2 key to display the appropriate Print Options.

Notes: The IA has a limited knowledge of the English language, therefore use words that are familiar. Records, field names, field values, built-in words, and words that you have taught it are items that the IA understands. To view the words the IA understands, press F6 to access the *See Words* command.

Requests that use the verbs "to be" and "to have" are easy for the IA to process. You could teach the IA new verbs, or rephrase the request to use "to be" or "to have." For instance, the sentence "Who sells in the Western Region?" could be rephrased as "Who are the salespeople in the Western Region?" to use the verb "to be."

The following is a list of some common requests which the IA can understand:

"**Calculate...**"—Requests which calculate arithmetic problems based on entered values, and field values (i.e., "Calculate 10 percent of the total sales." displays a report showing the total sales, and 10 percent of that number).

"**Change a Record...**"—Requests which modify data on a record or group of records (i.e., "Add $100,000 to the sales for the Western Region." will modify the database by adding $100,000 to the sales field for the record on which the region is Western).

"**Create a Record...**"—Requests which create a new record, or new records (i.e., "Add a new record with 'Ms. Brightwell' in the Manager field, and 'European' in the Region field." will add a new record with the specified fields filled in as quoted).

"Delete a Record..."—Requests which delete a record, or group of records (i.e., "Remove the records where the sales are less than $1,000,000." will delete the records on which the sales are less than $1,000,000).

"How Many..."—Requests which count the number of specified records (i.e., "How many states in the eastern region?" will produce a report counting the number of records for states in the eastern region).

"Run..."—Requests which run predefined reports, and Print Specs from the File Module. The request should be phrased as follows: "RUN *report* or *Print Spec name*."

"What..."—Requests which display selected fields, or calculate a specific value (i.e., "What are the sales of all states in the eastern region?" will produce a report displaying the total sales for all states in the eastern region).

"Where..."—Requests which display information on locations (i.e., "What is John Smith's residence?" will produce a report displaying John Smith's full home address if all fields making up the address are marked as being a location in the *Which Fields Contain Locations* command).

"Who..."—Requests which display information on people based on their characteristics (i.e., "Who earns more than Bob Smith?" will produce a report displaying the full names of those people who earn more than Bob Smith if all fields making up the names are marked as being a person's name in the *What Fields Contain People's Names* command).

Valid Keystrokes: F2—Once a report or record is displayed, to edit the Print Options and print

F6—See Vocabulary Words

Shift-F7—Restores the previous request

F8—Teach Vocabulary Words

See Also: *See Words* for information on seeing words the IA understands.

Teach Words for information on teaching the IA new words.

Columnar Report Questions for information on requests to create new columnar reports.

Cross Tab Report Questions for information on requests to create new cross tab reports.

Which Fields Contain Locations for information on specifying those fields that are locations.

What Fields Contain People's Names for information on specifying those fields that are names.

Print Options in the General Chapter for more information on setting these options.

_____ *Columnar Report Questions*

Menu Path: Assistant I Ask Me To Do Something

Description: IA requests that create columnar reports. Summary calculations can be included on these reports.

Procedure: 1. Begin the request with one of the following phrases:

```
Show...
List...
Report...
Get me a list...
```

Other phrases can be placed first, however these are common, and will be understood by the IA. Use any other phrases that are simple and make sensible replacements.

2. Specify which fields to include on the report. In addition to any fields you specify, the fields from the *Which Fields Identify a Form* command will be included on the report.

3. Optionally, specify any summary calculations to perform on the selected fields. To avoid confusing the IA, specify the summary calculations with the

fields in which to perform them (i.e., list average salary...—average is the calculation, and salary is the field).

4. Optionally, specify which records and in what sort order to include on the report. If you do not specify a group of records, the IA will assume that you want all records on the report.

5. Optionally, you can control which columns appear on the report. The IA will include any sort fields, calculation fields, fields used to restrict the records on the report, and fields that identify a form in the report. The following acronyms suppress the specified column:

WNIC—With no Identifying Columns.

WNRC—With no Restriction Columns.

WNEC—With no Extra Columns. Only displays the columns you explicitly ask for.

Notes: Predefined reports in the database can be run with the following request:

Run *REPORT NAME.*

If you have not specified any fields in the Which Fields Identify a Form command, the IA will not list the records in a report format. Instead it will try to display the records. You must have at least one field identifying a record.

Examples: The request:

List regions with expected sales greater than $1,000,000 and their managers sorted in descending order by sales.

displays all identifying columns, restriction columns (expected sales), and extra columns (sales).

See Also: *Selecting and Sorting Records in the IA* for information on specifying which records and in what order they should appear on the report.

Which Fields Identify a Form for information on specifying which fields should appear on all created reports.

Count... in the Query Guide

Menu Path: Assistant I Query Guide

Description: The first query fragment in a Query Guide request to count a group of selected records.

Procedure:
1. Select Count... from the Query Guide Request screen.

2. You will be presented with the following list of possible query fragments:

    The Records Where...—Retrieves a specified group of records for counting. The list of fields in the database will be displayed in the list box. Select one of the fields to use in selecting the group of records to count. The list of restriction query fragments will appear. Specify the restriction to place on the selected field. Once the restriction has been specified, you will have the option of specifying additional restrictions for this field, executing the request, or selecting additional fields for restriction.

    All the Records...—Retrieves all the records in the database for counting.

Notes: Once the request has been executed, the number of records in the selected group of records will appear in a report on the same screen (Query Guide Request screen). If you would like to print the report, press F2 to display the Report Print Options. To enter another request, press Escape.

Valid Keystrokes: Escape—Go to previous list of possible query fragments

F2—Once the count report is displayed, to print

F3—During the construction of request, to restart query building process

See Also: _Selecting and Sorting Records in the Query Guide_ for additional information on specifying which records to retrieve.

Print Options in the General Chapter.

Cross Tab Report Questions _____

Menu Path: Assistant | Ask Me To Do Something

Description: IA requests that create cross tab reports.

Procedure: 1. Begin the request with one of the following phrases:

```
Cross tab...
Cross Tabulate...
Cross-tabulate...
```

2. Specify which field to use as the summary field. If you would like to perform any calculations on the summary field, specify the type of calculation at this point. If you do not specify a calculation, the IA will use the default calculation for the data type of the summary field. See the *Cross Tab Spec* command in the Report Chapter for more information on the default calculations.

3. Follow the summary field with the keyword "by," and then specify which field to use as the row field. You may optionally specify a grouping for the rows, and the order in which to sort. To sort the row headings, insert either "ascending" or "descending" prior to specifying the field name depending on the required sort order. To group the records, follow the field name with "grouped by" and the type of grouping to use.

4. Follow the row field with the keyword "by," and then specify which field to use as the column field. You may optionally specify a grouping for the columns, and the order in which to sort. To sort the column headings, insert either "ascending" or "descending" prior to specifying the field name depending on the required sort order. To group the records, follow the field name with "grouped by" and the type of grouping to use.

Notes: Predefined reports can be run with the following request:

```
Run REPORT NAME.
```

Examples: The request:

```
Cross tab the average age by Hire Date
and by Sex.
```

displays a cross tab with age as the summary field (calculating the average), hire date as the row field, and sex as the column field.

See Also: *Cross Tab Spec* in the Report Chapter for additional information on cross tab reports.

_____ *Cross-Tabulate... in the Query Guide*

Menu Path: Assistant | Query Guide

Description: The first query fragment in a Query Guide request to create a cross tab report.

Procedure: 1. Select Cross-Tabulate... from the Query Guide Request screen.

2. You will be presented with the following list of possible query fragments:

All Statistics For ...—Based on the summary field type, calculates all applicable statistics from the following list:

Average for Number, and Money

Total for Number, and Money

Maximum for Number, Money, Date, Hour, Text, and Keyword

Minimum for Number, Money, Date, Hour, Text, and Keyword

Variance for Number, and Money

Standard Deviation for Number, and Money

Count of Values for Number, Money, Date, Hour, Text, and Keyword

The Average...—Calculates the average for the summary field. If you select this summary calculation, the summary field must be a numeric, or money field.

The Total...—Calculates the total for the summary field. If you select this summary calculation, the summary field must be a numeric, or money field.

The Maximum...—Calculates the maximum value for the summary field.

The Minimum...—Calculates the minimum value for the summary field.

The Variance...—Calculates the variance for the summary field. If you select this summary calculation, the summary field must be a numeric, or money field.

The Standard Deviation...—Calculates the standard deviation for the summary field. If you select this summary calculation, the summary field must be a numeric, or money field.

The Count of Values...—Calculates the count of values for the summary field.

If you select All Statistics..., skip to step 4.

3. Repeat step 2 for each calculation you would like to perform on the summary field. When all desired calculations have been chosen, select **For...** to continue.

4. The list of fields available for the summary field (the field to calculate as specified above) will appear. If you select **All Statistics..., The Total..., The Average..., The Variance...,** or **The Standard Deviation...** in step 3, the list will contain only numeric or money fields. Select the field to use as the summary field.

5. Select the sort order to use for the row field:

    By...—Sorts the row field in ascending order from top to bottom.

    By Decreasing...—Sorts the row field in descending order from top to bottom.

6. The list of fields in the database will appear for selection of the row field. Choose the field whose values you would like to provide the rows of the report. If you select a date field, choose one of the following time frames:

    Grouped by Year...—Groups records in a single row whose row field values are of the same year.

    Grouped by Month of the Year...—Groups records in a single row whose row field values are of the same month.

Grouped by Month...—Groups records in a single row whose row field values are of the same month and year.

Grouped by Day of the Month...—Groups records in a single row whose row field values are of the same day and month.

Grouped by Day of the Week...—Groups records in a single row whose row field values are of the same day of the week.

Grouped by Day...—Groups records in a single row whose row field values are of the same day, month, and year.

7. Select the sort order to use for the column field:

   By...—Sorts the column field in ascending order from left to right.

   By Decreasing...—Sorts the column field in descending order from left to right.

8. The list of fields in the database will appear for selection of the column field. Choose the field whose values you would like to provide the columns of the report. If you select a date field, group them by one of the available time frames.

9. Select one of the following query fragments to specify which records to include on the cross tab report:

   The Records Where...—Retrieves a specified group of records for the report. The list of fields in the database will be displayed in the list box. Select one of the fields to use in selecting the group of records to include in the report. The list of restriction query fragments will appear. Specify the restriction to place on the selected field. Once the restriction has been specified, you will have the option of specifying additional restrictions for this field, executing the request, or selecting additional fields for restriction.

   All the Records...—Retrieves all the records in the database for the report.

Notes: Once the report is displayed on screen, if you would like to print the report, press F2 to display the Report Print Options screen.

Even though you only have control over the way in which the Query Guide groups date values in the row or column field, it will try to group values as ranges for both numeric and monetary row or column fields. Text, keyword, and hour values in the row or column field will appear as individual rows or columns.

**Valid
Keystrokes:** Escape—Go to previous list of possible query fragments

F2—Once the report is displayed, to print

F3—Restart query building process

See Also: *Selecting and Sorting Records in the Query Guide* for additional information on specifying which records to retrieve.

Cross Tab Spec in the Report Chapter for additional information on the components of a cross-tab report.

Print Options in the General Chapter.

Defining Synonyms _____

Menu Path: Assistant I Ask Me To Do Something

Description: Defines a word or phrase to represent another word or phrase.

Procedure: 1. Type one of the following requests into the Ask Box to define a synonym:

Define *WORD* as *DEFINITION*.
Define *WORD* to be *DEFINITION*.
Define synonym.

or do one of the following to display the Synonym Definition screen from the IA Request screen:

Press F6 to See Words, and select Synonyms from the menu.

Press F8 to Teach Words, and select A Synonym from the menu.

2. Once at the Synonym Definition screen, type the synonym in the box on the left side of the screen, and type the definition in the box on the right side. To delete a synonym altogether, place the cursor on either side and press F3.

Notes: Synonyms are useful for defining short words or phrases to replace long words or phrases. They also are useful for defining words that do not fit in any of the IA's lessons.

Synonyms are only defined in the database being used in the IA at the time of the definition.

Examples: Define underpaid to be salary <= 20000.

The synonym defined (underpaid) will always be re-placed with the definition (salary <= 20000) for this database.

Valid Keystrokes: F3—At the Synonym Definition screen to delete a synonym

See Also: *Ask Me To Do Something* for information on the IA Request screen.

Find... in the Query Guide

Menu Path: Assistant | Query Guide

Description: The first query fragment in a Query Guide request to view and edit selected records that are optionally sorted.

Procedure:
1. Select **Find...** from the Query Guide Request screen.

2. You will be presented with the following list of possible query fragments:

The Records Where...—Retrieves a specified group of records, optionally sorted. The list of fields in the database will be displayed in the list box. Select one of the fields to use in selecting the group of records for viewing. The list of re-striction query fragments will appear. Specify the restriction to place on the selected field. Once the restriction has been specified, you will have the option of specifying additional restrictions for this field, executing the request, selecting additional fields for restriction, or specifying the sort order in which to view and edit the selected records.

All the Records...—Retrieves all the records in the database, optionally sorted. You will have the option of executing the request, or specifying the sort order in which to view and edit all the records.

The Current Record...—Retrieves the last record added.

Notes: Once the request has been executed, if any records meet the specified restrictions, you will be placed on the first record for viewing and editing. All keystrokes and commands available in Search/Update except Shift-F9 (Customize commands) are available for use.

**Valid
Keystrokes:** Escape—Go to previous list of possible query fragments

F2—Once a record is displayed, to print

F3—Restart query building process

See Also: *Selecting and Sorting Records in the Query Guide* for additional information on specifying which records to retrieve and in what order.

Search/Update in the File Chapter for information on available keystrokes and commands when viewing and editing the records.

Learn Values for Assistant _____

Menu Path: Assistant | Teach Me About Your Database | Learn Values for Assistant

Description: This onetime operation teaches all of the values in the database to the Assistant. If run again, this operation will "unteach" those values.

Procedure: 1. Select Learn Values for Assistant from the Basic
                        Lessons Menu.

                    2. If this is the first time you have run this operation
                        on this database, you will see a message indicat-
                        ing that Q&A will scan the database and record
                        all text values in a special index. Select YES from
                        the confirmation box.

                    3. If you have already taught the values to the As-
                        sistant for this database, then you will see a mes-
                        sage asking if you want to keep the values or de-
                        lete them. Select Keep the Values to quit without
                        modifying the index. Select Delete the Values if
                        you want to remove the index from the database.

Notes: It is not necessary to rerun this operation after add-
                    ing records. The Assistant automatically scans all text
                    fields as they are saved and stores the information
                    immediately.

                    Due to the extra work being done while records are
                    being saved, you may want to improve your data-
                    base's performance by "unteaching" the Assistant.

_____ *Produce a Report... in the Query Guide*

Menu Path: Assistant I Query Guide

Description: The first query fragment in a Query Guide request to
                    create a columnar report with selected fields and cal-
                    culations.

Procedure: 1. Select **Produce a Report Showing the...** from the
                        Query Guide Request screen.

                    2. You will be presented with a list of fields from the
                        database. Select a field to include on the report.

                    3. Select one of the following possible query frag-
                        ments. Depending on the type of field selected in
                        step 2, only some of these options may appear:

                    And the...—Allows the selection of additional
                        fields to include on the report. If you select this
                        option, you will not have an opportunity to
                        specify any calculations for the field selected in
                        step 2. If you select this option, return to step 2
                        to select the additional field.

From...—Allows the selection of records to include on the report. If you select this option, continue with step 4.

With Average...—Calculates the average of the values in the field selected in step 2.

With Total...—Calculates the total of the values in the field selected in step 2.

With Maximum...—Calculates the maximum value in the field selected in step 2.

With Minimum...—Calculates the minimum value in the field selected in step 2.

With Variance...—Calculates the variance of the values in the field selected in step 2.

With Standard Deviation...—Calculates the standard deviation of the values in the field selected in step 2.

With Count of Values...—Counts the nonblank values in the field selected in step 2.

If you select one of the calculation options, you will have the option to select from the remaining calculations for the field until either the **And the...** option to include another field, or the **From...** option to specify the records is selected.

4. Once all the fields to include on the report, and all the calculations to apply to these fields have been selected, the records to include on the report need to be specified. To do this you must select the **From...** option in step 3. The following query fragments are available:

The Records Where...—Retrieves a specified group of records, optionally sorted. The list of fields in the database will be displayed in the list box. Select one of the fields to use in selecting the group of records to include on the report. The list of restriction query fragments will appear. Specify the restriction to place on the selected field. Once the restriction has been specified, you will have the option of specifying additional restrictions for this field, executing the request, selecting additional fields for restriction, or specifying the sort order in which to include the records on the report.

All the Records...—Retrieves all the records in the database, optionally sorted. You will have the option of executing the request (placing a period at the end of the request), or specifying the sort order in which to include the records on the report.

The Current Record...—Retrieves the last record added for the report.

**Valid
Keystrokes:**   Escape—Go to previous list of possible query fragments

F2—Once the report is displayed, to print

F3—Restart query building process

See Also: *Selecting and Sorting Records in the Query Guide* for additional information on specifying which records to retrieve and in what order.

_____ *Query Guide*

Menu Path: Assistant | Query Guide

Description: The Query Guide allows English-like requests to be built for querying a database by offering lists of possible query fragments. Although requests in the Query Guide are limited in comparison to requests in the Intelligent Assistant, the Query Guide is faster in processing the requests.

Procedure: 1. Select Query Guide from the Assistant Menu.

2. Type the name of the database to query, and press Enter.

3. If the Query Guide has not been taught about this database, the "Read and Learn" dialog box will appear. If you would like to teach the Query Guide about this database, select YES. If you do not want to teach the Query Guide, select NO. If the database has no text or keyword fields, Q&A will ask you if you want to be prompted to teach the Query Guide as text or keyword fields are

added. For additional information see the *Teach Query Guide* command.

4. At the Query Guide Request screen you will see the following:

   Query Box—The box in which the query is built.

   Query Fragment List Box—The list of currently available query fragments.

   The following initial set of possible query fragments determines the type of request:

   Find...—Retrieves a specific set of records.

   Produce a Report Showing the...—Creates a detailed columnar report containing specific fields.

   Count...—Counts a specific set of retrieved records.

   Summarize the Data by...—Specifies the creation of a summary columnar report with statistical calculations on certain fields.

   Run...—Runs an existing Report or Print Spec.

   Cross-Tabulate...—Creates a cross tab report with row, column, and summary fields.

   Select the option that coincides with the type of request you would like to build, and press Enter. The selected query fragment will appear in the Ask Box. The list box will change to contain the possible query fragments to follow the option you chose. Continue selecting query fragments. As you select additional fragments, they will be added at the end of the current request in the Query Box.

5. Once the query has been built (signified by a period at the end of the sentence), it will be processed, and the appropriate action will be taken (i.e., a report will be created, or records will be viewed).

6. After the result of the query has been displayed, you may optionally press F2 to print it.

Notes: The Query Guide will behave slightly different when used with a database that hasn't been taught by the Query Guide. When a database has been taught, the Query Guide can prompt you with actual data values from text and keyword fields during the record selection process. Otherwise, you will be required to type in values.

At any time during the query building process, you may press F3 to clear the current request, and start again. You may also press Escape at any time to go to the previous list of requests.

Valid Keystrokes: Escape—Go to previous list of possible query fragments

F2—Print result of query

F3—Restart query building process

See Also: *Teach Query Guide* for additional information on how to teach the Query Guide.

Find... in the Query Guide for additional information on the possible query fragments after selecting this option.

Produce a Report... in the Query Guide for additional information on the possible query fragments after selecting this option.

Count... in the Query Guide for additional information on the possible query fragments after selecting this option.

Summarize... in the Query Guide for additional information on the possible query fragments after selecting this option.

Run... in the Query Guide for additional information on the possible query fragments after selecting this option.

Cross-Tabulate... in the Query Guide for additional information on the possible query fragments after selecting this option.

Selecting and Sorting Records in the Query Guide for information on selecting records to use in the appropriate request.

Print Options in the General Chapter.

Run... in the Query Guide

Menu Path: Assistant I Query Guide

Description: Runs an existing report or Print Spec from the database.

Procedure: 1. Select the Run... option from the initial list of query fragments.

2. Select one of the following possible query fragments from the next list:

   the Report...—Lists the available reports, both columnar and cross tab, from the database.

   the Print Spec...—Lists the available Print Specs from the database.

3. At the list of reports or Print Specs, select the one to run.

4. You will have the option to make temporary changes to the selected report or Print Spec. If you choose YES, you will be allowed to temporarily modify the specs and options that make up a report or Print Spec. If you choose NO, the report or print spec will run.

**Valid
Keystrokes:**   Escape—Go to previous list of possible query fragments

F2—Once the report is displayed, to print

F3—Restart query building process

See Also: *Design/Redesign a Report* in the Report Chapter for information on the specs and options that make up a report.

Design/Redesign a Spec in the File Chapter for information on the specs and options that make up a Print Spec.

See Words

Menu Path: Assistant I Ask Me To Do Something

Description: Displays the Assistant's built-in vocabulary, field names, and synonyms for the current database.

Procedure: 1. Press F6 from the IA Request screen.

2. Choose the type of words to display:

   Built-in Words—Displays a list of all the words the IA understands aside from the values and field names in the database.

   Field Names—Displays alternate field names for the IA, and optionally allows the addition or editing of alternate field names.

   Synonyms—Displays the current list of synonyms, and optionally allows the addition or editing of the synonyms.

See Also: *Alternate Field Names* for additional information on specifying field names.

Defining Synonyms for additional information on adding, or modifying synonyms.

___ *Selecting and Sorting Records in the Assistant*

Menu Path: Assistant I Ask Me To Do Something

Description: Describes the process of building a phrase to select and optionally sort records for IA requests.

Procedure: 1. To specify which records to include on the report, or view as a result of your request, use one of the following phrases prior to entering the actual restriction:

```
...where...
...on which...
...which...
...for...
...with...
...whose...
...have...
```

Other phrases can be used, however, these are common, and will be understood by the IA. Use any other phrases that are simple and make sensible replacements.

2. Follow the selected phrase with the name of the field (or alternate name) and the restriction to apply to the field. The restriction can be broken

down into two parts. The type of restriction and the restriction value. The type of restriction refers to how you want to restrict the data in the field and the restriction value refers to the restricting value for the field (i.e., in the phrase ...equals 1000..., equals is the type of restriction and 1000 is the restriction value). Table 5.2 is a list of the most common types of restrictions:

Table 5.2.   IA Restrictions

Restriction	Meaning	Example
=, Is, Equals >, Is Greater Than, Is After	equals; matches greater than; alphabetized after	Quantity = 1000 city > "New York"
<, Is Less Than, Is Before	less than; alphabetized before	State < "CA"
>=, Greater Than or Equal To, Is On or Later Than	greater than or equal to; appears in the alphabet at or later than	Dept >= "SALES" salary >= $30,000
<=, Less Than or Equal To, Is On or Later Than	less than or equal to; appears in the alphabet at or later than	date <= 10/1/91
/=, Is Not, Is Not Equal To	not equal	dept /= LEGAL
Top	closest to maximum	sales with top 5
Bottom	closest to minimum	sales with bottom 5
Begins with, Starts with	initial letters are	last name begins with "Jo"
Ends with	final letters are	last name ends with "son"
Contains	has within it the letters	last name contains "in"
Greatest	highest single value	region with greatest sales
Least	lowest single value	region with least sales
Earliest	oldest in a series of dates	earliest hire date
Latest	most recent in a series of dates	latest hire date

(continued)

Table 5.2. IA Restrictions *(continued)*

Restriction	Meaning	Example
Between	falls within	dept between sales and legal; dates between 4/5/91 and 10/5/91
Not	negates the next item	dates not between 4/5/91 and 10/5/91

3. Optionally, you may sort the records for the request. After you have specified the restrictions to apply, enter one of the following phrases:

```
...sorted by...
...sorted by descending...
```

The IA defaults to an ascending sort unless you explicitly ask for a descending sort. Enter the name of the field for the primary sort.

4. If you have additional fields to sort on, enter one of the following phrases:

```
...and by...
...and by descending...
```

Enter the name of the additional field. Repeat this step until all sorts are specified.

Notes: There are many ways to phrase a restriction for records you would like included in a request. This command touches on the common restrictions. Using words that have been taught to the IA (synonyms, locations, people's names, verbs, adjectives) can make the process of selecting a group of records easier.

Examples: Restrictions appear in italics, whereas sorting appears underlined.

Show regions *where sales > $1,000,000.*

List *female* employees *with salary greater than or equal to $30,000* <u>sorted by Dept.</u>

For the male employees, list the cities *where the alma mater is Stanford,*

<u>sorted by state, and by descending</u>
<u>city.</u>

See Also: *What Fields Contain People's Names*

Which Fields Contain Locations

Advanced Vocabulary : Adjectives

Advanced Vocabulary : Verbs

Selecting and Sorting Records in the Query Guide

Menu Path: Assistant | Query Guide

Description: The process of building phrases in the Query Guide
to select and optionally sort records for requests. The
query fragments described in this command are
available from most of the initial query fragments
(i.e., **Find...**, **Count...**, etc.) except for the **Run...**
fragment.

Procedure: 1. To access the selection and sorting fragments, one
of the following fragments should have been se-
lected from the specified query:

   The Records Where...—Select this from the
   Find..., **Produce a Report Showing the...**, and
   Count... queries.

   From the Records Where...—Select this from the
   Summarize the Data by..., and **Cross-Tabulate...** queries.

2. Choose a field from the list of fields in the database to use in restricting the records for the query.

3. A list of restrictions for the selected field will appear. The field type, and whether the Query
Guide has been taught or not will affect the list of
possible constraints. Select one of the restrictions
in Table 5.3 to apply to the field selected in step 2:

Table 5.3.   QG Restrictions

Restriction	Description
Text/Keyword Field Type	
Equals...	Lists the data values found in the field. Selects only records with the chosen value in the field. Appears only if the selected field has been taught to the Query Guide.
Begins With...	Allows the input of a sequence of characters. Selects only records on which the field begins with the entered sequence of characters.
Ends With...	Allows the input of a sequence of characters. Selects only records on which the field ends with the entered sequence of characters.
Contains...	Allows the input of a sequence of characters. Selects only records on which the field contains the entered sequence.
Matches...	Allows the input of a sequence of characters. Selects only records on which the field equals the entered sequence.
Matches the SOUNDEX Pattern...	Allows the input of a sequence of alphabetic characters. Selects only records on which the field sounds like the entered sequence.
Appears Alphabetically...	Selects only records on which the field value meets one of the following alphabetic constraints: Before...—Allows the input of a word that should be greater than the field value. After...—Allows the input of a word that should be less than the field value. First...—The field value should be the lowest Last...—The field value should be the highest. Among the...—Allows the input of a number (*n*) specifying the highest or lowest *n* field values.
Does Not...	Negates of one of the constraints above.
Is...	Selects only records on which the field value meets one of the following format constraints: Empty...—The field should not have a value. Not Empty...—The field should contain a value.

(continued)

Table 5.3.   QG Restrictions (*continued*)

Restriction	Description
	Correctly Formatted...—The field should contain a correctly formatted value.
	Incorrectly Formatted...—The field should contain an incorrectly formatted value.
Number/Money Field Type	
Is...	Allows the input a numeric value. Selects only records on which the field equals the entered number.
Is Greater Than...	Allows the input of a numeric value. Selects only records on which the field is greater than the entered number.
Is Less Than...	Allows the input of a numeric value. Selects only records on which the field is less than the entered number.
Is At Least...	Allows the input of a numeric value. Selects only records on which the field equals or is greater than the entered number.
Is At Most...	Allows the input of a numeric value. Selects only records on which the field equals or is less than the entered number.
Is the...	Selects only records in which the field value meets one of the following constraints:
	Greatest...—The field value is the greatest of all the records.
	Least...—The field value is the least of all the records.
Is Among the...	Allows the input of a number (n) specifying those records with the greatest or least n field values.
Is Empty...	Selects only records on which the field has no value.
Is Correctly Formatted...	Selects only records on which the field value is correctly formatted.
Is Not...	Negates one of the constraints above.
Date/Time Field Type	
Is...	Allows the input of a date/time value. Selects only records on which the field equals the entered date or time.

(*continued*)

Table 5.3. QG Restrictions *(continued)*

Restriction	Description
Is After...	Allows the input of a date/time value. Selects only records on which the field is greater than the entered date or time.
Is Before...	Allows the input of a date/time value. Selects only records on which the field is less than the entered date or time.
Is the...	Selects only records in which the field value meets one of the following constraints: Earliest...—The date/time is the oldest of all the records. Latest...—The date/time is the most recent of all the records.
Is Among the...	Allows the input of a number (*n*) specifying those records with the oldest or most recent *n* dates/times.
Is Empty...	Selects only records on which the field has no value.
Is Correctly Formatted...	Selects only records on which the field value is correctly formatted.
Is Not...	Negates one of the constraints above.

4. Once the restriction has been specified, select one of the following query fragments:

   And the...—Allows restrictions to be placed on additional fields. If you select this option, continue with step 2.

   .—Ends and processes the request.

   Sorted by...—(Only for **Find...** and **Produce a Report Showing the...** requests) Sorts, in ascending order, the selected records for the query. Selecting this option will display a list of the fields from the database. After choosing a field to sort on, the following list of query fragments will be displayed:

   And by...—Allows ascending sorts to be placed on additional fields.

   And by Decreasing...—Allows descending sorts to be placed on additional fields.

   .—Ends and processes the request.

> **Sorted by Decreasing...**—(Only for **Find...** and
> **Produce a Report Showing** the... requests)
> Sorts, in descending order, the selected records
> for the query. Selecting this option will display
> a list of the fields from the database. After
> choosing a field to sort on, the following list of
> query fragments will be displayed:
>
> > **And by...**—Allows ascending sorts to be placed
> > on additional fields.
> >
> > **And by Decreasing...**—Allows descending sorts
> > to be placed on additional fields.
> >
> > **.**—Ends and processes the request.
>
> **Or...**—Allows additional constraints to be placed
> on the field. If you select this option continue
> with step 3.

Valid Keystrokes:	Escape—Go to previous list of possible query fragments
	F3—Restart query building process
See Also:	*Retrieve Spec* in the File Chapter for additional information on the meaning of the different types of retrieval.
	Format Values in the File Chapter for additional information on the different field types.

Summarize... in the Query Guide _____

Menu Path:	Assistant I Query Guide
Description:	The first query fragment in a Query Guide request to create a report summarizing specified statistics for a selected group of records.
Procedure:	1. Select the **Summarize the Data by...** option from the Query Guide Request screen.
	2. A list of all the fields in the database will appear. Select the primary field to summarize.
	3. Choose one of the following possible query fragments:

> **And by...**—Select another field to summarize. Additional summary fields are subgroups of the

primary field. Summary calculations for these fields will appear within the constraints of the primary field. Continue with step 2.

Showing the...—Specifies the summary calculation to apply to a field yet to be specified. Continue with step 5.

Showing All Statistics For ...—Based on the field type, calculates all applicable statistics from the following list:

Average for Number, and Money

Total for Number, and Money

Maximum for Number, Money, Date, Hour, Text, and Keyword

Minimum for Number, Money, Date, Hour, Text, and Keyword

Variance for Number, and Money

Standard Deviation for Number, and Money

Count of Values for Number, Money, Date, Hour, Text, and Keyword

From the list of available fields, select the one on which to perform the calculations. Skip to step 6.

4. If you chose **Showing the...** in step 3, select one of the following summary calculations:

Average...—Averages the values in the field to be specified. If you choose this option, the field to summarize must be a number or money field.

Total...—Totals the values in the field to be specified. If you choose this option, the field to summarize must be a number or money field.

Maximum...—Finds the maximum value in the field to be specified.

Minimum...—Finds the minimum value in the field to be specified.

Variance...—Calculates the variance in the field to be specified. If you choose this option, the field to summarize must be a number or money field.

Standard Deviation...—Calculates the standard deviation in the field to be specified. If you choose this option, the field to summarize must be a number or money field.

Count of Values...—Counts the records with a value in the field to be specified.

5. Repeat step 4 until all desired calculations have been chosen. To continue select the **For...** option. At the list of available fields, choose the one on which to apply the calculations.

6. Choose one of the following possible query fragments:

And...—Allows the specification for summary calculations on additional fields. If you chose the **Showing All Statistics for...** option in step 3, see that section in step 3. If you chose the **Showing the...** option, see that section in step 3.

From the Records Where...—Retrieves a specified group of records. The fields in the database will be displayed in the list box. Select one of the fields to use in selecting the group of records for the summary report. The list of restriction query fragments will appear. Specify the restriction to place on the selected field. Once the restriction has been specified, you will have the option of specifying additional restrictions for this field, executing the request, or selecting additional fields for restriction.

All the Records...—Retrieves all the records in the database.

Valid Keystrokes: Escape—Go to previous list of possible query fragments

F2—Once the summary report is displayed, to print

F3—Restart query building process

See Also: *Selecting and Sorting Records in the Query Guide* for additional information on specifying which records to retrieve.

_____ *Teach Me About Your Database*

Menu Path: Assistant I Teach Me About Your Database

Description: Used to teach the IA what the database is about, and what words you will use to refer to fields so that the IA can better understand your requests.

Procedure: 1. Select Teach Me About Your Database from the Assistant Menu.

2. Type the name of the database you want to teach and press Enter. If the database has never before been used with the Assistant, the Assistant will pause to learn its built-in words, plus the database's spec names, and field names.

3. The Basic Lessons Menu displays the following options:

   Learn Values for Assistant—This onetime operation teaches all of the values in the database to the Assistant. If run again, this operation will "unteach" those values.

   What this Database Is About—Teach the Assistant words that describe what your records represent.

   Which Fields Identify a Form—Specify which fields should be included in all reports to identify the record.

   Which Fields Contain Locations—Indicate which fields contain places.

   Alternate Field Names—Teach different names for your fields.

   Advanced Lessons—Accesses lessons to teach the Assistant specific adjectives, verbs, units of measure, and the locations of peoples names.

See Also: *Learn Values for Assistant*
What This Database Is About
Which Fields Identify a Form
Which Fields Contain Locations
Alternate Field Names
Advanced Lessons

Teach Query Guide _____

Menu Path: Assistant | Teach Query Guide

Description: Teaches the Query Guide about the specified database so that actual field data from text or keyword
fields can be presented in the list box for use during
the record selection query stage.

Procedure: 1. Select Teach Query Guide from the Assistant
Menu.

2. Type the name of the database to teach, and press
Enter.

3. Type a Q into each text or keyword field you
would like to teach the Query Guide. You can
press F5 to place a Q in every field.

4. Press F10 when you have finished.

Notes: The Query Guide will learn values only in text or
keyword fields. The values from these fields will be
listed during the query building process if, for example, you are selecting records for a report. For additional information see the *Selecting and Sorting Records in the Query Guide* command.

Text fields must be single line fields with less than 60
characters. The process of teaching the Query Guide
basically indexes the field values for all selected
fields. This allows faster retrieval of records during
processing of requests. If you have many text or keyword fields, teaching the Query Guide about a lot of
these fields may slow down data entry, since Q&A
needs to index every piece of data for every selected
field.

If you do not have any text or keyword fields, you
may still want to teach the Query Guide; that way, if
you add text or keyword fields later, the Query
Guide will ask if you want it to "read and learn"
them.

The database can be "untaught" by removing the Q
from any or all the fields.

Valid
Keystrokes: F5—Place a Q in all fields

See Also: *Selecting and Sorting Records in the Query Guide* for information on how taught fields affect the selection process.

_____ *Teach Words*

Menu Path: Assistant I Ask Me To Do Something

Description: Teaches the Assistant various types of words that can then be used in requests.

Procedure: 1. Press F8 from the IA Request screen.

2. Choose the type of word to teach the IA from the following list:

   A Word for the Subject of the Database—Words that describe what each record in the database contains. The command, *What This Database Is About*, displays the same screen as this option.

   A Field Name—Alternate names for fields in the database. The command *Alternate Field Names* displays the same screen as this option.

   A Synonym—A word that can have the same meaning as another word. The command *Defining Synonyms* discusses the Synonym Definition screen.

   A Verb—A word that can replace the phrase "has a _____ of" (i.e., for the field address, the phrase "has an address of" is the same as the verb "lives") and thereby simplify the request. The command *Advanced Vocabulary: Verbs* displays the same screen as this option.

   Other—Suggestions on how to proceed if the word to teach is not one of the previous types.

See Also: *What This Database Is About* for additional information on teaching the IA the subject of the database.

Alternate Field Names for additional information on teaching the IA alternate names for fields.

Defining Synonyms for additional information on defining synonyms.

Advanced Vocabulary: Verbs for additional information on teaching the IA verbs to associate with specific fields.

Units of Measure _____

Menu Path: Assistant I Teach Me About Your Database I Advanced Lessons I Units of Measure

Description: Teaches the Assistant which unit of measure (e.g., inches, pounds, miles) you will use with each numeric field.

Procedure: 1. Select Units of Measure from the Advanced Lessons Menu.

2. If the database has no number fields, you will not be able to proceed because Units of Measure can only be defined for numeric fields. See *Format Values* in the File Chapter to change your field's information type.

3. Use F6 and F8 to select the previous or next number field for which you want to define units of measure.

4. Type a unit of measure for the selected field. Repeat steps 3 and 4 until finished.

5. Press F10 to continue.

Example: | Field | Units |
| --- | --- |
| A person's age | years |
| A distance | miles, kilometers, inches |
| A weight | pounds, ounces, grams |

**Valid
Keystrokes:**   F6—Select previous number field

F8—Select next number field

See Also: *Format Values* in the File Chapter to change your field's information type.

What Fields Contain People's Names _____

Menu Path: Assistant I Teach Me About Your Database I Advanced Lessons I What Fields Contain People's Names

Description: Teaches the Assistant which fields contain all or part of people's names.

Procedure: 1. Select What Fields Contain People's Names from the Advanced Lessons Menu.

2. Move to a field that contains a person's whole name or part of the name (i.e., first name, last name, etc.).

3. Type a number that is unique to that name. Each part of a compound name must have the same number.

4. Follow the number with one of the following letters to indicate which part of the name it is:

   W—Whole name. Use this letter if the field contains the entire name.

   T—Title. Use this letter if the field contains only the person's title (e.g., Mr., Mrs.).

   F—First name. Use this letter if the field contains only a person's first name.

   M—Middle name. Use this letter if the field contains only the person's middle name.

   L—Last Name. Use this letter if the field contains only the person's last name.

   S—Suffix. Use this letter if the field contains only the person's suffix (e.g., Ph.D., Jr.).

5. Repeat steps 3 and 4 for each name in the database.

6. Press F10 to save the information.

7. If you specified any name fields, the first one will be highlighted. Enter the name that you will use to refer to this person in requests to the Assistant. You may also enter alternate field names for this person. Press F6 and F8 to select the previous or next name field. Press F10 when finished.

Valid Keystrokes: F6—Select previous name field while teaching alternate field names

F8—Select next name field while teaching alternate field names

See Also: *Alternate Field Names* to define alternate field names to other fields.

What This Database Is About _____

Menu Path: Assistant I Teach Me About Your Database I What This Database Is About

Description: Teaches the Assistant words that describe what your records represent.

Procedure: 1. Select What Is This Database About from the Basic Lessons Menu.

2. Type one or more words that complete the sentence, "Each record contains information about a particular _____."

3. Press F10 when finished.

Notes: The words taught here may be used in questions that refer to the forms.

Examples: Your records might represent people, employees, books, cars, etc.

If your database is about books, you could use the word "book" in requests to the Assistant, e.g., "Which books were written by Herman Melville?"

Which Fields Contain Locations _____

Menu Path: Assistant I Teach Me About Your Database I Which Fields Contain Locations

Description: Teaches the Assistant which fields contain places or locations.

Procedure: 1. Select Which Fields Contain Locations from the Basic Lessons Menu.

2. If there are fields that contain locations, number them in the order you want them to appear in reports. These columns will appear each time you ask the Assistant for a location. You can have up to eight location columns.

3. Press F10 to continue.

Which Fields Identify a Form

Menu Path: Assistant I Teach Me About Your Database I Which Fields Identify a Form

Description: Specify which fields are necessary to identify a form, and should therefore be included in all reports.

Procedure:
1. Select Which Fields Identify a Form from the Basic Lessons Menu.

2. If there are columns that are needed to identify a record, then they should be included in each report from the Assistant. Type a 1 in the first field that identifies the form. This field will appear as the first column in all reports from the Assistant. If necessary, type a 2 in the second field that identifies the form. It will appear as the second column. You may have up to eight identification columns.

3. Press F10 to continue.

See Also: _Columnar Report Questions_ for more information on excluding identification columns from reports.

6

Utilities

Several Q&A commands that are not done on a regular basis but are necessary for the operation of Q&A can be found in this chapter. These include installing a printer, setting global options (i.e., default database and document paths), and modifying Q&A font description files.

Copy a File

See *DOS File Facilities*

Delete a File

See *DOS File Facilities*

DOS File Facilities

Menu Path: Utilities I DOS File Facilities

Description: Allows files to be listed, renamed, deleted, and copied.

Procedure: 1. Select DOS File Facilities from the Utilities Menu.

2. The DOS File Facilities Menu displays the following choices:

   List Files—List specified files in a subdirectory.

   Rename a File—Renames a file to new name.

   Delete a File—Deletes a file.

   Copy a File—Copies a file to a another name.

3. Select the operation to perform.

4. If you chose to rename, delete, or copy a file, type the name of the file and press Enter. If you chose to list files, type the name of the subdirectory for which you want to list the files and press Enter.

You may additionally include DOS wildcards to limit the number of files that are displayed.

5. If you chose to rename or copy a file, type the new name and press Enter.

Install Printer

Menu Path: Utilities | Install Printer

Description: Allows the installation of printers connected to either the parallel ports (i.e., LPT1, LPT2, LPT3) or the serial ports (i.e., COM1, COM2) of your computer.

Procedure:

1. Select Install Printer from the Utilities Menu.

2. At the Printer Selection screen, select the Q&A printer to install or change.

3. At the Port Selection screen, choose the destination for the output:

   LPT1, LPT2, LPT3—Sends output to one of the parallel ports in your computer.

   COM1, COM2—Sends output to one of the serial ports in your computer.

   FILE—Saves output (including printer control codes) in a file on disk.

   FAX0—Sends output to an Intel SatisFAXtion or Connection Coprocessor fax board, if installed in your computer.

4. If you selected a parallel port, serial port, or disk file as the destination from step 3, skip to step 5. If you selected the FAX0 option, the following Special Port Options will be displayed:

   FAX1 Intel Connection: Fine Res/80 Columns—Produces 200 $\times$ 200 dots per inch, with 80 characters across, and 66 lines per page.

   FAX2 Intel Connection: Fine Res/132 Columns—Produces 200 $\times$ 200 dots per inch, with 132 characters across, and 88 lines per page.

   FAX3 Intel Connection: Standard Res/80 Col—Produces 200 $\times$ 100 dots per inch, with 80 characters across, and 66 lines per page.

FAX4 Intel Connection: Standard Res/132 Col—
Produces 200 × 100 dots per inch, with 132
characters across, and 88 lines per page.

Choose the appropriate option for the type of
output desired. Continue with step 11.

5. Select the manufacturer of your printer from the
List of Printer Manufacturers, and press Enter.

6. Select your printer model from the list of supported printers, and press Enter. Your choice of
model will be confirmed, and Q&A will display
any special information about the chosen printer.

7. Press Enter to confirm your selection and go to
step 11. Optionally, press F8 to set the Special
Printer Options.

8. If you selected LPT1, LPT2, LPT3, or FILE for
the port in step 3, then skip to step 9. If you selected COM1 or COM2, set the following COM
(Serial) Port Settings:

Baud Rate—This is the speed at which the data
to be printed will be sent to your printer. The
default is 9600.

Data Bits—This is the number of bits representing a character that your printer is expecting.
The default is 8.

Stop Bits—This is the number of bits sent to your
printer that represent a stop. The default is 1.

Parity—This determines if data sent to your
printer should be transmitted with additional
bits to make the total number odd or even.
The default is NONE.

These options should match those expected by
your printer. Press F10 when you have finished
with these settings.

9. The Special Printer Options allow you to set the
following options:

Check for Printer Timeout?—The timeout is the
length of time Q&A will wait for the printer to
respond to commands. If you select YES, Q&A
will display the message "Printer not respond-
ing" if the printer does not respond in the

specified time. If you select NO, Q&A will
continue to try to print without displaying a
message. The default is YES.

Length of Timeout (in seconds)—This is the
length of the timeout (the above option). The
default is 15 seconds. This value is ignored if
the above option is NO.

Check for Printer Ready Signal?—Q&A will
check for a printer ready signal from your
printer, and if none is received, display a
"Waiting for printer" message if this option is
YES. The default option is YES.

Check for Paper Out?—Q&A will check for a pa-
per out signal from your printer, and display a
"Waiting for printer" message if this option is
YES. The default option is YES.

Formfeed at End of Document?—Setting this option to YES forces the printer to eject the last
page of a document. The default option is NO.

Font File Name—This is the name of the font file
Q&A expects to use with this printer. Documents attempting to use another font file
while printing will use this one instead.

After setting the Special Printer Options,
press F10.

10. The More Special Printer Options screen will be
displayed. For those options requiring a printer
control code, enter the numeric ASCII equivalents of the control codes separated by commas,
or press Alt-F10, and then hold down the Alt
key while entering the numeric value of the
ASCII character on the numeric keypad. The actual character should appear. Set any of the following options:

Bin 1 through Bin 3 Setup Code—These are the
codes that tell Q&A to use paper from a particular bin. You may select from up to three
bins if installed on your printer, and the correct codes have been entered.

Eject Page Code—This is the code to send to the
printer to eject the last page during printing.

Start of Document Code—This is the code to send to the printer at the beginning of printing.

End of Document Code—This is the code to send to the printer at the end of the printing.

Envelope Height—This is the number of line feeds to send when you have selected the Envelope Line Spacing option from the Write Print Options. The default is 24.

11. Q&A will confirm the installation of your printer, and ask if you would like to install another printer. If you answer YES, return to step 3.

Notes: You may install up to five printers in Q&A. This allows multiple printers, or a single printer with several modes to be installed.

If you do not see your printer manufacturer or model, consult your printer manual to see if your printer can emulate one of the supported manufacturers or models.

**Valid
Keystrokes:**   F8—At the list of printer models to set the printer options

F9—At the COM (Serial) Port Settings, Special Printer Options, and More Special Printer Options to reselect the printer

See Also: *Print Options* in the General Chapter for information on the Envelope Line Spacing option.

List Files _____

See *DOS File Facilities*

Modify Font File _____

Menu Path: Utilities I Modify Font File

Description: Allows the creation and modification of font description files which Q&A uses to access and use fonts during printing.

Procedure:

1. Select Modify Font File from the Utilities Menu.

2. Type the name of the new font file to create, or the existing font file to modify.

3. If you are adding a font description to a new font file, continue with step 4.

   If you are modifying an existing font description, use the F9 and F10 key to move backward and forward through the font description records until the one to modify is displayed.

   If you are adding a font description to an existing font file, press F8 to display a blank font description screen to fill in.

   If the font being added is similar to an existing font in the file, find the existing font description, and press Shift-F5 to copy it. The copy will be placed at the end of the file, where you may then modify it as you require.

4. At the Modify Font Description screen add or modify the following values:

   Font Name—This is the name of the font; it is displayed on the Font Assignment screen.

   Printer Name—This is the name of the printer with which this font will be used; it is displayed on the Font Assignment screen.

   Abbreviation—This is an abbreviation for the font name; it is displayed on the Font Assignment screen, the Text Enhancements and Fonts Menu, and on the status line when the cursor is on any text formatted with this font. It may be up to six characters in length.

   On Codes—These are the codes sent to your printer to turn on a font. Font codes are dependent on the hardware/software (i.e., font cartridges, soft fonts, etc.) used to generate fonts on your printer. Consult your printer manual, or information that accompanied your cartridge or soft fonts for the appropriate On Codes.

   Off Codes—These are the codes sent to your printer to turn off a font. Font codes are dependent on the hardware/software (i.e., font cartridges, soft fonts, etc.) used to generate fonts

on your printer. Consult your printer manual,
or information that accompanied your cartridge
or soft fonts for the appropriate Off Codes.

Point Size—This is the height of the font. For regular proportional or nonproportional fonts, enter a number from 1 to 999. Type an E for enhancements, or S for scalable font. Neither of
these has an associated point size. Q&A uses
the point size to calculate the space to leave
between lines of text. If the point size is 1 to
14, the spacing is 1. For every increment of 12
points, the spacing is increased by 1. For a scalable font, you may control the spacing yourself,
by following the S with the number of spaces
to leave between lines of text.

Characters per Inch—This is the number of characters that will fit in one inch horizontally. For
nonproportional spaced fonts, enter the fixed
number of characters per inch. For proportional
spaced and scalable fonts, enter a P; if this is
an enhancement, enter an E.

Printer Resolution—This is the number of dots
per inch that your printer can print. Consult
your printer manual for this information. You
must fill in this field if the current font is a proportional or scalable font.

Character Width Table—This represents the table
of width values for the ASCII characters. Width
information is dependent on the font being
added/modified. Consult your printer manual,
or information that accompanied your cartridge
or soft fonts for the character widths. You must
fill in the widths for the characters you want to
use if the current font is a proportional or scalable font.

5. Press F10 to save the options entered and view
the next font description, or Shift-F10 to save the
options entered and exit.

Notes: Enhancements are used to modify the attributes of
the printed font (e.g. boldface or italics), and not the
actual font.

To specify a scalable font, make sure you have an S in the Point Size field, and that an asterisk (*) is used in the On Code field in place of the point size. This signifies that Q&A will replace the asterisk with the point size at print time.

Valid Keystrokes:
F3—Delete the current font description

Shift-F5—Copy the current font description to the end of the file

F8—Add a new font description to the file

F9—Display the previous font description

F10—Display the next font description

See Also:
Font Assignments in the General Chapter for information on assigning fonts for use.

Text Enhancments and Fonts Menu in the General Chapter for information on selecting assigned fonts for use.

Rename a File

See *DOS File Facilities*

Set Alternate Programs

Menu Path: Utilities I Set Alternate Programs

Description: Allows up to six programs or macros to be installed on the Q&A Main Menu for execution as another Q&A menu item.

Procedure:
1. Select Set Alternate Programs from the Utilities Menu.

2. You have the option of entering up to six alternate programs or macros that can be executed from the Q&A Main Menu. Each new menu item requires two pieces of information:

   Alternate Program—The path and name of the alternate DOS program (i.e., C:\LOTUS\123.COM), or the keystroke of a Q&A macro (e.g., alta).

Menu Selection—The name (up to 13 characters) you want to see on the Q&A Main Menu to represent the alternate DOS program or macro from above.

Notes: At the Q&A Main Menu, the alternate program or macro can be selected by pressing the first character of the Menu Selection option.

Only macros that have a key identifier of Alternate A–Z (e.g., alta) can be used.

See Also: *Q&A Main Menu* in the General Chapter for information on activating the Alternate Programs.

Define Macro in the Macros and Menus Chapter for information on the key identifier for a macro.

Set Global Options

Menu Path: Utilities I Set Global Options

Description: Sets options for use throughout the entire product, including pathnames for database, document, and temporary files, the current network ID, and automatic execution of menu options.

Procedure: 1. Select Set Global Options from the Utilities Menu.

2. At the Set Global Options screen set the following options:

Q&A Document Files—Type the pathname to appear when Q&A prompts for a document. At any prompt for a word processing document, Q&A will use this path as the default (this can be changed to access documents in other directories). The default is the directory in which Q&A is installed.

Q&A Database Files—Type the pathname to appear when Q&A prompts for a database. At any prompt for a database, Q&A will use this path as the default (this can be changed to access databases in other directories). The default is the directory in which Q&A is installed.

Q&A Temporary Files—Type the pathname to use for any temporary files Q&A needs to create. Temporary files are created for use by Q&A, and then deleted when no longer needed. The default is the directory in which Q&A is installed.

Automatic Execution—Determines how Q&A will execute menu selections. If you select YES, menu items will automatically be executed when the selection's single key selection character is pressed (i.e., at the Q&A Main Menu, pressing F will automatically display the File Menu). If it is NO, then you must press Enter after pressing the single-key selection character.

Network ID—Sets your user name to display during operations on a network by many users on a database. This name is displayed to inform another user if you have locked part or all of a database.

See Also: *Q&A on a Network* in the General Chapter for information on multi-user and single-user database operations.

7

Macros and Menus

Macros are a way to record and play back repetitive keystrokes. They can be used to type a simple sentence in the word processor or automate complex reporting procedures.

Custom Menus can be used to personalize Q&A's Menu Structure to suit your needs. You can create menus that are displayed at the touch of a button, that add to or replace an individual Q&A menu, or that replace all Q&A menus with a complete structure of your own.

This chapter explains all of the available macro and menu operations.

The word "Macro" in the Menu Path of a command means the Macro Menu. You can display the Macro Menu at any time by pressing Shift-F2.

Application Menu Options _____

Menu Path: Macro | Create Menu

Description: Controls all aspects of a Custom Menu, including the items that appear on the menu, the actions of each item, and how the menu is displayed.

Procedure: 1. Once at the Application Menu Options screen, set the following options:

     Menu Name—This is the internal name used when referring to this Custom Menu. If the name is the same as a Q&A menu name, then the Custom Menu will be a Replacement Menu. You may press Alt-F7 to view and select from a list of Q&A Menu names.

     Display—Full Screen menus will appear on the screen by themselves. Overlay menus appear on top of the text already on the screen. Replacement Menus will not be displayed the same as the menus they are replacing. For example, if you replace the File Menu you will not be able to see the Q&A Main Menu "behind" it.

Status—Controls whether the menu can be displayed. Active indicates that it can be used, while Inactive indicates that the menu cannot be displayed.

Menu Returns—A setting of YES tells Q&A to return to this Custom Menu when finished with the selected macro. For example, if a macro selected from this menu takes the user to Add Data for a certain database, then the return to this menu will take place when the user leaves Add Data. If a macro runs a complete procedure, such as printing a few records, and finishes on a Q&A menu, then you will immediately return to this Custom Menu. When you are returned to this menu because the Menu Returns setting is YES, the underlying Q&A menu is the Q&A Main Menu. With Menu Returns set to NO, all macros selected as options from this menu end without returning to this menu.

On Escape, Show Menu—When building menu structures, this option indicates which menu, if any, you would like to display when a user is viewing this menu and then presses Escape. If this option is left blank, pressing Escape while viewing this Menu will cancel this menu, but will not display another. You may press Alt-F7 to view a list of the currently defined Custom Menus.

Menu Title—This is the title of the menu that will appear on the top line of the menu, above the solid separator line. This does not have to be the same as the Menu Name, and is not the name by which this menu will be accessed.

Items 1–9—These are the selections that will appear on the custom menu itself. Type them exactly as you want them displayed. If the first letter of the item is capitalized, then that item will automatically be selected when the user presses that letter. If the Global Option, Automatic Execution is set to YES, the chosen selection is automatically executed, otherwise you must press Enter after pressing the letter of the selection.

Macro Names—These are the names of the macros or menus that will be executed when the corresponding item is selected. Putting the name of a macro executes the macro, while putting the Menu Name of a Custom Menu displays the menu. You may press Alt-F7 to display a list of currently defined macros and menus.

Valid Keystrokes: F2—Preview the menu

Alt-F7—List of options

See Also: *Set Global Options* in the Utilities Chapter to set the Automatic Execution option.

Using Custom Menus

Clear Macros _____

Menu Path: Macro I Clear Macros

Description: Clears the currently loaded macro file from memory.

Procedure: 1. Press Shift-F2 to display the Macro Menu.

2. Select Clear Macros from the Macro Menu.

Notes: All currently loaded macros will be cleared from memory. Once macros have been cleared, they will no longer be available for use in the current session of Q&A, unless they are loaded again using the Get Macros command.

See Also: *Get Macros* for information on loading macros.

Create Menu _____

Menu Path: Macro I Create Menu

Description: Creates customized menus that may be used throughout Q&A. You can create Custom Menus that can be viewed at the touch of a button, you can add to or replace any individual Q&A menu, or replace all Q&A menus with a complete structure of your own.

Procedure:
1. Press Shift-F2 to display the Macro Menu.
2. Select Create Menu and press Enter.
3. From the list of currently defined Custom Menus, choose --- New Menu --- to create a new Custom Menu, or select the name of a menu to edit. Press Enter to continue.
4. Set the Application Menu Options as desired, then press F10 to continue.
5. When prompted to Save Macros to File, type the name of the macro file in which you want to store this Custom Menu, then press Enter.

See Also: *Application Menu Options* for descriptions of the various settings available from that screen.

Using Custom Menus

Define Macro

Menu Path: Macro I Define Macro

Description: Allows the creation of macros through "live" recording of keystrokes.

Procedure:
1. Press Shift-F2 to display the Macro Menu.
2. Select Define Macro from the Macro Menu.
3. For the macro being created, press the key identifier to be associated with this macro, or press Enter for none. If you select a key identifier that is used by another macro, Q&A will ask if you would like to overwrite that macro.
4. Q&A will display a flashing box in the lower-right corner of the screen to indicate that you are recording the macro. All further keystrokes will be saved in the macro in the order executed.
5. To pause the macro for variable input (i.e., if you want to type in the name of a file that will be different every time the macro is run), press Alt-F2. The cursor will change to a flashing square, and Q&A will prompt you to enter the variable keystrokes. Keystrokes entered at this time will not be

saved in the macro. After entering the variable keystrokes, press Alt-F2 to continue the recording of the macro.

6. After all keystrokes for the macro have been entered, press Shift-F2 to stop the recording of the macro.

7. At the Macro Options box, enter the following:

   Macro Name—The name of the macro can be up to 31 characters in length. Initially, it will default to the key identifier in step 2 if one was entered. Changing the name will not change the key identifier. If you use the name of an existing macro, Q&A will ask if you want to overwrite that macro. The macro name is required.

   Show Screen—This option determines whether Q&A will update the screen, showing the effects of the macro when it is executed. If you select YES, the screen will be updated as the macro runs. If you select NO, the screen will not change until the macro is complete, at which point the final state of the screen after the keystrokes will be displayed. If the macro contains a pause and this option is set to NO, once the pause is encountered the screen will update until the end of the macro.

   End with Menu—Optionally, enter the name of a Custom Menu that this macro should display upon completion. Press Alt-F7 to display a list of available Custom Menus.

8. After setting the options, press F10. You will be prompted to save your macro to the current macro file. Press Enter to save the macro to this file, or enter the name of a new macro file in which to save all loaded macros.

Notes: If the macro name is "center button," or "right button," the macro can be run using the center or right button on your mouse.

Macros can be "nested" up to five levels deep. This means that one macro may call another macro, and so on up to five levels of calls.

Pressing Escape when Q&A prompts to save the macro to disk, will not delete the macro from memory. The macro will still be available for use until Q&A is exited, at which point it will no longer exist. If you use the Save Macros command before exiting Q&A, the macro will be saved.

Valid
Keystrokes: Alt-F2—Pauses a macro for input of variable keystrokes

Alt-F7—At the Macro Options dialog box to display a list of available Custom Menus

See Also: *Save Macros* for information on saving macros to a disk file.

Run Macro for information on running recorded macros.

Create Menu for information on creating custom menus.

Delete Macro

Menu Path: Macro I Delete Macro

Description: Deletes an existing macro from memory.

Procedure: 1. Press Shift-F2 to display the Macro Menu.

2. Select Delete Macro from the Macro Menu.

3. At the list of Macro Names, select the macro to delete. The selected macro will be removed from memory.

4. Type the name of the file in which to save the macros remaining in memory, and press Enter.

Notes: If you choose to save the macros remaining in memory to the same file from which they were loaded, the deleted macro will no longer exist anywhere. If you only want to delete the macro from memory temporarily, press Escape when prompted to save macros.

Get Macros _____

Menu Path:	Macro I Get Macros
Description:	Loads into memory an existing macro file from disk.
Procedure:	1. Press Shift-F2 to display the Macro Menu.
	2. Select Get Macros from the Macro Menu.
	3. Type the name of the macro file to load, and press Enter.
Notes:	Upon starting Q&A the default macro file, QAMACRO.ASC, is loaded (if it exists). Command Line Loading options allow you to load macros from a different file upon starting Q&A. To load macros from another file for only one session of Q&A, use the -AL option, followed by the name of the macro file. To load macros from another file for every session of Q&A, use the -AD option, followed by the name of the macro file.
	Only one macro file may be loaded in memory at any one time. If you load a different macro file using this command, the previously loaded macro file (if any) is removed from memory.
	Macro files can be up to 30,000 characters in length. If you try and load a macro file that exceeds this limit, Q&A will display an error message referring to the number of the macro at which it ran out of memory.
See Also:	*Command Line Loading Options* in the General Chapter for information on loading alternate macro files upon starting Q&A.

Macro Menu _____

Menu Path:	Macro
Description:	Displays the Macro Menu that contains commands to manipulate and modify macros and custom menus.
Procedure:	1. Press Shift-F2 from anywhere in Q&A, except Page Preview.
	2. At the Macro Menu, the following options will be displayed:

Run Macro—Executes an existing macro.

Define Macro—Allows "live" recording of a macro.

Delete Macro—Deletes an existing macro from memory.

Get Macros—Loads into memory a macro file from disk.

Save Macros—Saves the currently loaded macros to a file.

Clear Macros—Removes the macros currently in memory.

Create Menu—Allows the creation of custom menus.

See Also: *Run Macro*

Define Macro

Delete Macro

Get Macros

Save Macros

Clear Macros

Create Menu

_____ *Macro Options*

See *Define Macro*

_____ *Protect Macro File*

Menu Path: File I Design File I Customize Application I Protect Macro File

Description: Encrypts a macro file so that it cannot be edited.

Procedure: 1. Select Protect Macro File from the Customize Application Menu.

2. Type the name of the macro file you want to encrypt and press Enter.

3. Type the name you want the encrypted macro file to have. This name should be different from the editable macro file name in step 2. If you enter

the same name, then the editable copy of your macro file will be lost. In its place will be one that cannot be edited.

4. Press Enter when both file names are correct.

Notes: A protected macro file can be used just like any other macro file, except that once a protected macro file is in use, pressing Shift-F2 displays a list of the available macros, instead of the Macro Menu. Consequently, you cannot perform the functions on the Macro Menu (e.g., Delete Macro, Define Macro, Save Macros, etc.).

Once a macro in a protected macro file is started, it cannot be interrupted with the Escape key.

In a protected macro file, all macros that have names which begin with an "at-sign" (@) will not appear on the list of available macros. These excluded macros can only be run from a Custom Menu.

See Also: *Macro Menu*

Creating Menus for information on creating Custom Menus.

Run Macro _____

Menu Path: Macro I Run Macro

Description: Executes a macro from a list of macro names.

Procedure: 1. Move to the place in Q&A that the desired macro is designed to start from and press Shift-F2 to display the Macro Menu.

2. Select Run Macro from the Macro Menu.

3. Select the desired macro from the alphabetized list, and press Enter. The macro will begin to execute. If the Macro Option Show Screen is set to NO, then you will see a flashing message "Macro working...."

Notes: There are several other ways to execute macros:

Keystroke Identifier—If the macro was defined with a keystroke identifier (e.g., Alt-A), then pressing the keystroke will start the macro.

Alt-F2—You may display the alphabetized list of
macros to execute by pressing Alt-F2.

Right Button—A macro may be associated with
the Right Button of your mouse. Pressing the
Right Button on the mouse will immediately
execute that macro. If you have a three-button
mouse, you may also associate a macro with
your Center Button. If a macro has not been
defined for the Right Button of your mouse,
pressing it will also display the list of macros,
and choosing one will execute it. You cannot
associate a macro with the Left Button of your
mouse.

Alternate Program—You can install a macro as an
Alternate Program. This macro must have a
keystroke identifier of Aiternate A–Z.

Custom Menu—A macro may be installed as a selection from a Custom Menu.

Autostart Macros—Macros can be started as soon
as a user loads Q&A; these macros are called
Autostart Macros. An Autostart Macro must
have a keystroke identifier of Alternate 0–9.
The macro is executed by loading Q&A with
the Command Line Option -m#, where # is the
number of the macro identifier (i.e., -m3 executes Alt-3). See *Command Line Loading Options* in the General Chapter for more information about this option.

See Also: *Define Macro*

Set Alternate Programs in the Utilities Chapter for
information about installing Alternate Programs.

Create Menu for information about creating Custom
Menus.

Command Line Loading Options in the General
Chapter for more information about the option -m#.

_____ *Save Macros*

Menu Path: Macro I Save Macros

Description: Saves the currently loaded macros to a disk file.

Procedure: 1. Press Shift-F2 to display the Macro Menu.

2. Select Save Macros from the Macro Menu.

3. Type the name of the disk file in which to save the macros currently in memory. Q&A will display the currently loaded macro file as the default. If none is loaded, no default will appear.

Notes: Saving macros to a disk file does not remove them from memory. Once macros have been saved to a disk file, they can be loaded at any future time using the Get Macros command.

See Also: *Get Macros* for information on loading macros.

Using Custom Menus _____

Custom Menus can be used to personalize Q&A's Menu Structure to suit your needs. You can create menus that are displayed at the touch of a button, that add to or replace an individual Q&A menu, or that replace all Q&A menus with a complete structure of your own. Each of these different types of Custom Menus requires different settings on the Application Menu Options Screen, so it is important to decide which type of menu is correct for your application before you begin using them.

Pop-Up Menus—The first type of menu is displayed at the end of a macro. A macro can be defined that, when finished, displays a custom menu containing selections that can run other macros. This type of menu, called a Pop-Up Menu, might be useful in the word processor. It could display macro selections that type standard introductions and conclusions to your documents.

After defining all of the macros that should appear on the menu and making sure that they all begin from the same location in Q&A, use the command *Create Menu* to install those macros onto a menu with the following Application Menu Options:

Menu Name—This name should not be the name of a Q&A menu.

Display—This should be set to Overlay.

Menu Returns—This setting must be NO.

On Escape, Show Menu—This line should be left blank.

Then define one more macro with the keystroke that should display the Pop-Up Menu (e.g., Alt-M). Immediately press Shift-F2 to end the macro recording, and set the Macro Options screen with these settings:

Macro Name—This can be any name that you want.

Show Screen—This should be set to YES.

End with Menu—This line must be the Menu Name of the Pop-Up Menu. Press Alt-F7 for a list of Menu Names and select the correct one.

Replacement Menu—The second type of Custom Menu is called a Replacement Menu. These menus actually replace one of the Q&A menus. Consequently, you may remove and rearrange the items on a Q&A menu as well as add more macro selections. Items on the Q&A menu are "removed" when there is no choice from the Replacement Menu that executes that option. For example, you may want to restrict users from accidentally using Remove or Design File from the File Menu. You can replace as many Q&A menus as you want, and each time that Q&A menu would be displayed, your Replacement Menu will appear instead. Use the *Create Menu* command to create a Replacement Menu with the following Application Menu Options:

Menu Name—This should be the name of the Q&A menu you want to replace. Press Alt-F7 to view a list of all Q&A Menu Names.

Display—This should be Full Screen.

Menu Returns—This setting must be NO.

On Escape, Show Menu—This line should be left blank.

Macro Name—These are the names of the macros corresponding to the items on the menu. All macros on a Replacement Menu must be defined to start from the menu being replaced. To access one of the options on the Q&A menu being replaced, enter the letter of that option as the Macro Name.

Replacement Menus offer many new capabilities, but they do have several limitations. You are locked into the existing Q&A menu structure. You may exclude certain menu choices and even exclude some menus altogether, but you cannot add any new menus. You may add items to existing Q&A menus, but you are limited to nine total items per menu. These limitations are all overcome by Custom Menu Structures.

Custom Menu Structures—The last type of menu is actually a set of menus that are "connected" into a treelike structure. One Custom Menu may contain selections that call other Custom Menus, and pressing Escape from these menus can return you to the first menu. There is no limit to the number of separate menus that can be included in a Custom Menu Structure.

There are two different ways to access a Custom Menu Structure after it is designed. You may design the top level of your structure as a Pop-Up Menu that can be chosen as an Alternate Program from the Q&A Main Menu. The structure then is called a Supplemental Menu Structure, because all of the Q&A menus are still available, but the structure is also available as a supplemental set of menus. The second way to access your Custom Menu Structure is to make the top level of your structure a Replacement Menu for the Q&A Main Menu. This replaces the real Q&A Main Menu with the top of your structure. This Replacement Menu Structure is the only set of menus that a user can view. None of the Q&A menu choices are available directly. Consequently, every function must be accessed using a macro selection on one of the menus. If you are creating a Replacement Menu Structure, you must be sure that all macros function properly from each menu, and that the menus are "connected" in the correct fashion.

Custom Menu Structures offer the most flexibility in terms of their design and implementation, but they are also the most complex of the three types of Custom Menus. Consequently, if a menu structure is necessary for your application, you should design it one menu at a time, testing all functions before continuing. This will help identify any problems while they can still be corrected easily.

To create a Custom Menu Structure, design all of the menus in the structure using the *Create Menu* command and set the following Application Menu Options on each of the menus:

Menu Name—This must not be a replacement name (i.e., the name of a Q&A menu).

Display—This must be set to Full Screen.

Menu Returns—This must be set to YES for all menus in a Custom Menu Structure.

On Escape Show Menu—This line should contain the name of the custom menu you want displayed when the user presses Escape from the current menu. This option gives the menus their hierarchical or treelike structure.

Items 1–9 and **Macro Names**—All selections must be either run a macro or display a Custom Menu. Single keystrokes for the Macro Name, designed to execute a command on the underlying Q&A menu, will not work properly on Custom Menu Structures. All macros in a Custom Menu Structure must be defined to start from the Q&A Main Menu. To create an option on a custom menu which displays a submenu, enter the Menu Name of the submenu as the Macro Name for the appropriate item.

To design your Custom Menu Structure as a Supplemental Menu Structure, simply create a macro like that used for Pop-Up Menus to "pop-up" the top menu of your structure. To design it as a Replacement Menu Structure, simply make the top menu of the structure a Replacement Menu for the Q&A Main Menu by setting its Menu Name to "Q&A Main Menu".

See Also: *Define Macro* to define the macros that will appear as selections on your Custom Menus.

Create Menu for general information about creating menus.

Application Menu Options for more detailed descriptions about these options.

8

Programming

Q&A has an extensive built-in programming language that can be used in many different operations. In addition to programming executed during addition or modification of records, programming may be used to update a group of selected records, retrieve a group of selected records, create derived columns and fields on reports, or in mail merge documents.

This chapter provides information on all the predefined functions in Q&A, and their uses. Each command contains a list of operations in which it is available. The possible areas are shown in Table 8.1:

Table 8.1. Areas Available

Command	Abbreviation
Program Form	Program
Mass Update	Update
Field Navigation	Navigation
Retrieve Spec	Retrieve
Merge Document Programming	Merge
Derived Columns	Derived
Derived Fields	Derived
Initial Values	Initial Values

@ABS(Number)

Program, Update, Navigation, Retrieve, Merge, Derived

Description: Finds the absolute value of Number.

Parameters: **Number**—This is an expression that should evaluate to the number of which to take the absolute value.

Notes: This function can be abbreviated as @AB. The parameter remains the same.

_____ *@ADD*

See *Context Functions*

_____ *@ASC(String)*

Program, Update, Navigation, Retrieve, Merge, Derived

Description: Returns a number that represents the ASCII decimal equivalent of the first character of String. @ASC returns 0 if String is empty.

Parameters: **String**—This should be an expression that evaluates to a text string.

Notes: This programing function can be abbreviated as @AS. All of the parameters remain the same.

Examples: @ASC("dogs and cats")

Returns 100 because the ASCII decimal equivalent of "d" is 100.

See Also: *@CHR* to return a character when given its ASCII decimal equivalent.

_____ *@AVG(List)*

Program, Update, Navigation, Retrieve, Merge, Derived

Description: Calculates the average of the values in the List.

Parameters: **List**—This is a comma-delimited (i.e., separated by commas) list of expressions that should evaluate to numeric or monetary values. A range of Field Ids (e.g., #10, #11, #12, and so on through #20) may be represented with two periods between the lowest and highest Field Ids (e.g., #10..#20). A range of Field Names that differ due only to a unique number at the end of the name (e.g., Test1, Test2, Test3, and so on through Test10), may also be separated by two periods and included in the list (e.g., Test1..Test10).

Notes: This function can be abbreviated as @AV. The parameter remains the same.

If one of the expressions evaluates to a blank value (i.e., a field with no value), it is not included in the calculation.

Examples: To average a list of 10 students' test scores with fields numbered from #100 to #200:

```
Student Average = @AV(#100..#200)
```

CEND _____

See *Navigation Statements*

@CGR(Present Value, Future Value, Number of Periods) _____

Program, Update, Navigation, Retrieve, Merge, Derived

Description: Calculates the compounded growth rate (i.e., rate of return) of an investment based on Present Value, Future Value, and the Number of Periods.

Parameters: **Present Value**—This is an expression that should evaluate to the present value of the investment. The sign should be the same as Future Value.

Future Value—This is an expression that should evaluate to the future value of the investment. The sign should be the same as the Present Value.

Number of Periods—This is an expression that should evaluate to the number of periods over which to determine the rate of return. This must be a positive value, and cannot be zero.

Notes: This function returns the rate of return as a decimal value. To convert the return value to a percentage, multiply it by 100.

The formula that Q&A uses for this calculation is:

```
CGR = ((Future Value / Present Value) ^
(1/Number of Periods)) - 1.00
```

Examples: The following will find the compounded growth rate (#40) of an investment of $5,000 (#10) today, worth $10,000 (#20) in 24 months (#30):

```
#40 = @CGR(#10, #20, #30) * 100
```

This will result in a compound growth rate of 2.93 percent (note the multiplication by 100 to convert to a percentage).

_____ *CHOME*

See *Navigation Statements*

_____ *@CHR(Number)*

Program, Update, Navigation, Retrieve, Merge, Derived

Description: Returns the character whose ASCII decimal equivalent is the specified Number.

Parameters: **Number**—This should be an expression that evaluates to a number. The number must be between 1 and 254.

Notes: This programing function can be abbreviated as @CH. All of the parameters remain the same.

Examples: @CHR(81) + @CHR(38) + @CHR(65)

Returns the letters "Q&A" because the ASCII decimal equivalent of "Q" is 81, and so on.

See Also: *@ASC* to return the ASCII decimal equivalent of a character.

_____ *CLEAR(List)*

Program, Update

Description: Blanks the field values of the fields in the List.

Parameters: **List**—This is a comma-delimited (i.e., separated by commas) list of expressions that should evaluate to numeric or monetary values. A range of Field Ids (e.g., #10, #11, #12, and so on through #20) may be written with two periods between the lowest and highest Field Ids (e.g., #10..#20). A range of Field Names that differ due only to a unique number at the end of the

name (e.g., Test1, Test2, Test3, and so on
through Test10), may also be separated by two
periods and included in the list (e.g.,
Test1..Test10).

Examples: CLEAR(Salary, Bonus, #10..#36)

Blanks the Salary and Bonus fields and Field IDs
numbered 10 through 36.

CNEXT _____

See *Navigation Statements*

Context Functions _____

Description: These functions are used to determine the "mode"
(either Add Data or Search/Update) in which Q&A is
being used. The following are the available context
functions:

> **@ADD**—Checks if you are using Add Data.
>
> **@UPDATE**—Checks if you are using Search/Up-
> date.

Notes: These functions are used as the condtion to meet in
an IF..THEN..ELSE statement. They can be most ef-
fective if you want certain programming to occur
only when you are in Add Data or Search/Update.

See Also: *IF..THEN..ELSE* for information on constructing this
type of statement.

Add Data and *Search/Update* in the File Chapter

CPREV _____

See *Navigation Statements*

@DATE _____

Program, Update, Navigation, Retrieve, Merge, Derived, Initial

Description: Returns the current date from the system clock.

Notes:	This programing function can be abbreviated as @DA.
	If the system clock is not accurate, then @DATE will return incorrect dates.
Examples:	Date of Sale: Date of Sale = @DATE
	Puts the current date into the Date of Sale field.
See Also:	*@TIME* to return the current time from the system clock.

_____ *@DEL(Field, Start Position, Number)*

Program, Update, Navigation, Retrieve, Merge, Derived

Description:	Returns Field with Number characters removed starting from Start Position.
Parameters:	**Field**—This is the text from which to delete characters. It can be any expression.
	Start Position—This should be an expression that results in a number. It represents the position of the first character in Field to delete.
	Number—This should be an expression that results in a number. It represents the number of characters to delete.
Notes:	This programing function can be abbreviated as @DE. All of the parameters remain the same.
	If the Start Position is less than or equal to 0 then the deleting will start with the first character of the Field. If Start Position is a number greater than the length of Field then no deleting will take place.
	If the Number is less than or equal to 0 then no deleting will be done.
Examples:	@DEL("Q&A Command Reference", 4, 8)
	Returns "Q&A Reference" because " Command" was deleted.

_____ *@DITTO(List)*

Program

Description: Copies the contents of the fields in the List from the previous record into those same fields on the current record. This statement works only during Add Data.

Parameters: **List**—This is a comma-delimited (i.e., separated by commas) list of expressions that should evaluate to numeric or monetary values. A range of Field Ids (e.g., #10, #11, #12, and so on through #20) may be written with two periods between the lowest and highest Field Ids (e.g., #10..#20). A range of Field Names that differ due only to a unique number at the end of the name (e.g., Test1, Test2, Test3, and so on through Test10), may also be separated by two periods and included in the list (e.g., Test1..Test10).

Notes: This programing statement can be abbreviated as @DI. All of the parameters remain the same.

Examples: @DITTO is a statement, not a function. Therefore, it does not return any value to be assigned to another field.

City: < City = @DITTO(City)

is not legal. Instead, use the following:

City: < @DITTO(City)

@DOM(Date) _____

Program, Update, Navigation, Retrieve, Merge, Derived

Description: Returns a number representing the day of the month of Date.

Parameters: **Date**—This is any expression that evaluates to a date.

Notes: This programing function can be abbreviated as @DM. All of the parameters remain the same.

Examples: @DOM("June 17, 68")

returns the number 17 because the specified date is the 17th day in the month.

_____ *@DOW$(Date)*

Program, Update, Navigation, Retrieve, Merge, Derived

Description: Returns the text string of the day of the week of Date.

Parameters: **Date**—This is any expression that evaluates to a date.

Notes: This programing function can be abbreviated as @DW. All of the parameters remain the same.

Examples: In Mail Merge Programming:

...when we spoke last *program {@DOW$ (Last Contact)}*, I assumed you were ready to sell...

Replaces the Print Command, Program with the day of the week for the date in the Last Contact field.

See Also: *Print Commands* in the Write Chapter for more information about Mail Merge Programming.

_____ *@ERROR*

Program, Update, Navigation

Description: Returns TRUE if the most recent XLOOKUP command failed, or FALSE if it was successful or there was no XLOOKUP.

Notes: This error checking function will return TRUE for @XLOOKUP, XLOOKUP, @XLOOKUPR, and XLOOKUPR if no matching record was found or the return value was blank.

Examples: To display a message if an error occurred during the most recent XLOOKUP:

#10 : IF @ERROR THEN @MSG("The XLOOKUP was unsuccessful!")

See Also: *Xlookup Functions and Statements*

@MSG for information on displaying a message in a programming statement.

IF..THEN..ELSE

@EXP(Number, Power) _____

Program, Update, Navigation, Retrieve, Merge, Derived

Description: Raises Number to the Power degree.

Parameters: **Number**—This is an expression that evaluates to a numeric value to be raised.

   Power—This is an expression that evaluates to the degree to which to raise the Number.

Notes: This function can be abbreviated as @EX. The parameters remain the same.

Examples: To find the number of square feet in a sq. mile (5,280 feet in a mile):

   #10 = @EXP(5280,2)

   The resulting value (#10) will be 27,878,400 sq. feet.

@FIELD(Expression) _____

Program, Update, Navigation, Retrieve, Merge, Derived

Description: Returns a field reference that can be used in place of any Field ID or Field Name. This field reference is derived from Expression and must return either the text of a Field Name or the number of a Field ID.

Parameters: **Expression**—This should be an expression that returns a text string of a Field Name or a Field ID. If a text value is returned, Q&A looks for a field with a matching Field Name. If none was found, Q&A converts the text value to numerals and looks for a matching Field ID. If a number value is returned, Q&A immediately looks for a matching Field ID.

Notes: The abbreviated form of this function is the "at-sign" (@) followed by Expression in parenthesis, (i.e., @(Expression)). Expression is evaluated the same way.

   If no matching Field Name or Field ID can be found, the reference is undefined. If the undefined @FIELD reference was used to provide a field reference for use as the destination for the results of a statement (i.e., the left side of a statement), that statement does not have any effect. For example, the statement:

`@FIELD("Salary") = 3 + 4`

would normally assign the value 7 to the salary field. If there were no Salary field, the statement would have no effect.

If an undefined @FIELD reference is used as the value part of a statement (i.e., the right side of a statement), the returned value is "ERR". For example, the statement:

`Salary = @FIELD("Bonus")`

would normally assign the value of the Bonus field to the Salary field. If there were no Bonus field, the value "ERR" is assigned to the Salary field.

Expression can be a text string (e.g., @FIELD("Salary")), a simple expression (e.g., @FIELD(5 + 2)), a Field ID or Field Name (e.g., @FIELD(Region), or a complex expression (e.g., @FIELD(@MONTH$(DATE))).

Examples: To assign a deposit amount to a different total field depending on the month that the deposit was made, use the following statement:

`@FIELD( @MONTH$( Deposit Date ) + " Tot-`
`al" ) = Deposit`

If the Deposit Date is May 3, 1986, this statement assigns the Deposit amount to a field named May Total.

See Also: *@MONTH$* for more information about returning the month name of a date.

_____ *Field Names and Field IDs*

Description: Programming statements are widely used to operate on data in a database. To do this, a means of specifying which field's data to use in the operation is necessary.

Field Names and Field IDs are used to specify which field's data to use in a calculation.

A Field Name is the name of the field specified in the *Set Field Names* command of the File Chapter.

You may use this name to specify a field in a programming statement in all areas where programming is available.

A Field ID, sometimes called a Logical Field Number (LFN), is a number which you assign to a field. The number is preceded by the pound sign (#), and can be used to identify fields in all areas where programming is available.

Notes: Field Names containing nonalphabetic or nonnumeric characters (e.g., .,;/?) should be specified as #"Field Name".

See Also: *Set Field Names* in the File Chapter for information on specifying the internal field names.

@FILENAME _____

Program, Update, Navigation, Retrieve, Merge, Derived

Description: Returns the complete path and filename of the current database.

Notes: This programing function can be abbreviated as @FN. All of the parameters remain the same.

Examples: To use XLOOKUP to look into the current file:

XLOOKUP(@FILENAME, #1, "Acct No", "Minimum Balance", #2)

See Also: *Xlookup Functions and Statements*

@FV(Payment, Interest, Number of Payments) _____

Program, Update, Navigation, Retrieve, Merge, Derived

Description: Calculates the future value of an investment based on the Payment amount, the Interest rate per payment, and the Number of Payments.

Parameters: **Payment**—This is an expression that should evaluate to the amount of each payment.

         Interest—This is an expression that should evaluate to the interest rate per payment. This value must be greater than or equal to -1, and should be expressed as a decimal value. To convert from a percentage to a decimal value, divide by 100.

Number of Payments—This is an expression that should evaluate to the number of payments made for the investment.

Notes: The formula that Q&A uses to calculate the future value is:

FV = Payment * (((1 + Interest) ^ (Number of Payments) - 1.00) / Interest)

Examples: The following will find the future value (#40) of an investment based on a monthly payment of $100, an interest rate of 1% per month over a period of 5 years:

#40 = @FV(100, 1 / 100, 5 * 12)

The future value (#40) will be $8166.97.

_____ *GOSUB Field*

Program

Description: Creates a programming subroutine by transferring program control to another field until a RETURN statement is executed. Upon executing a RETURN statement, control is returned to the field that began the subroutine, and execution continues with the statements immediately following the GOSUB command.

Parameters: **Field**—This can be any Field ID or Field Name. The field must contain On Field Entry programming and a RETURN statement.

Notes: Instead of a RETURN statement, the field that is referenced by the GOSUB command may contain any Navigation Statement as long as the field referenced by the Navigation Statement contains On Field Entry programming and a RETURN statement.

If the field referenced by the GOSUB command does not contain On Field Entry programming, or does not contain a RETURN command, an error will be displayed at the time the programming is executed.

Examples: The following is an example of a programming sub-
                 routine using GOSUB and RETURN:

```
Amount 1: > Amount 1 = Amount 1 * 1.25;
          GOSUB Total; CNEXT

Amount 2: > Amount 2 = Amount 2 * 1.25;
          GOSUB Total; CNEXT

Amount 3: > Amount 3 = Amount 3 * 1.25;
          GOSUB Total

Total: < Total = @SUM( Amount 1..Amount
3 ); RETURN
```

After leaving the Amount 1 field, the programming
statements in that field are executed. First the value
of Amount 1 is increased by 25%, then the subroutine begins. The subroutine totals the three
amount fields and then RETURNS to the CNEXT
statement following the GOSUB command in
Amount 1. The CNEXT statement moves the cursor
to the Amount 2 field. Each Amount field performs
similar operations. The advantages of this system are
that the lengthy statement in the Total field had to be
written only once, and if it needs to be changed it
only has to be changed in one place.

See Also: *RETURN*

                 Navigation Statements for more information on pro-
                 gramming commands that control the movements of
                 the cursor.

GOTO Field _____

See *Navigation Statements*

@GROUP _____

See *Multi-user Functions*

@HELP(Field) _____

Program, Navigation

Description: This statement displays the Custom Help Screen for Field. If Field does not have a Custom Help Screen, then @Help has no effect. The user can press Escape to clear the help screen.

Parameters: **Field**—This can be any Field ID or Field Name.

Notes: If the Help Mode is set to Concurrent through the Define Custom Help command, then @Help will have no effect when used as an On Field Exit Statement.

Examples: `<#11: IF Commission > 10 THEN @HELP( Commission )`

See Also: *Define Custom Help* in the File Chapter for information on creating custom help screens and setting the Help Mode.

_____ *IF...THEN...ELSE*

Program, Update, Navigation

Description: An IF...THEN...ELSE or conditional statement allows you to control the execution of certain programming statements based on a condition. If the condition is met, then Q&A will execute a specified statement or set of statements. Optionally, another statement or set of statements can be executed if the condition is not met.

The syntax for this type of statement is:

`IF <condition> THEN <statement> [ ELSE <alternate statement> ]`

The keywords IF and THEN must appear exactly as above, and in the same order. Each part of the statement is defined as follows:

   <condition>—This is any valid expression that evaluates to TRUE or FALSE. If <condition> is TRUE, then <statement> will be executed. If <condition> is FALSE, then execution of the statement is complete. If <condition> is FALSE, and the optional ELSE clause has been used, then <alternate statement> will be executed.

<**statement**>—This is any valid statement that you would like to execute if <condition> is TRUE.

[**ELSE...**]—This is an optional clause of an IF...THEN...ELSE statement beginning with the keyword ELSE. Following ELSE is <alternate statement> that is any valid statement to execute if <condition> is FALSE.

Notes: Both <statement> and <alternate statement> can be more than one valid statement. If you would like to execute multiple statements, then use the following syntax:

```
IF <condition> THEN {<statement1>;
<statement2>;...} [ ELSE {<alternate
statement1>; <alternate statement2>;...} ]
```

Note that both <statements> and <alternate statements> are separated by semicolons (;) and are enclosed in braces. The braces can be replaced by the keywords BEGIN and END respectively.

The operators AND, OR, and NOT can be used as a part of <condition> to test for more complex conditions. Use AND if you would like to use multiple conditions and want them all to be met (e.g., IF State = "CA" AND Sales Rep = "Jim Riley"... will execute <statements> only if State is CA and Sales Rep is Jim Riley). Use OR if you would like to use multiple conditions, and require that at least one is met (e.g., IF Zip Code = "95014" OR Zip Code = "94040"... will execute <statements> if Zip Code is either 95014 or 94040). Use NOT to "negate" the condition; in other words if the condition is TRUE, make it FALSE, and vice versa (e.g., IF NOT Dept = "SALES"... will execute <statements> only if Dept is not SALES).

Examples: `IF Dept = "LEGAL" THEN Bonus Factor = 7.9`

This will set the Bonus Factor field to 7.9 only if the Dept field contains LEGAL.

```
IF Dept = "SALES" AND Region = "Eastern"
THEN {Contact = "John Gibson"; Contact
Phone = "(510)555-3443"}
```

This will set the Contact field to John Gibson, and the Contact Phone field to (510)555-3443 only if the Dept field is SALES and the Region is Eastern.

@INSTR(Field, String)

Program, Update, Navigation, Retrieve, Merge, Derived

Description: The "In String" function returns a number representing the position of String in Field. If String appears
multiple times in Field, the returned number will be
the position of the first occurrence.

Parameters: **Field**—This should be an expression.

String—This is the text whose position will be returned. It can be any expression.

Notes: This programing function can be abbreviated as @IN.
All of the parameters remain the same.

@INSTR returns 0 if the String does not appear in
the Field.

Examples: `@INSTR("hot air balloon", "a")`

Returns the number 5 because the first "a" is in the
5th position.

@INSTR can be used as a parameter for many other
text and string functions, for example:

`@LEFT(Whole Name, @INSTR(Whole Name,
" "))`

Returns all the letters up to the first space (i.e., the
first name) no matter where the space is located.

See Also: *@LEFT* to return the leftmost characters of a field.

@INT(Number)

Program, Update, Navigation, Retrieve, Merge, Derived

Description: Returns only the integer, and not the fractional part,
of Number.

Parameters: **Number**—This is an expression that should evaluate to the numeric value of which to take only
the integer portion.

Notes: This function can be abbreviated as @IT. The parameter remains the same.

Examples: On a Retrieve Spec:

{@INT(Interest Rate) = 10}

This will find all the records on which the interest rate is in the range from 10 through 11 (e.g., 10, 10.2, 10.5, 10.99).

@IR(Present Value, Payment Amount, Number of Payments)

Program, Update, Navigation, Retrieve, Merge, Derived

Description: Calculates the interest rate of a loan based on Present Value, Payment Amount, and Number of Payments.

Parameters: **Present Value**—This is an expression that should evaluate to the amount of the loan left to pay.

Payment Amount—This is an expression that should evaluate to the payment made per period.

Number of Payments—This is an expression that should evaluate to the number of payments made for the investment.

Notes: The return value (interest rate) is in decimal form. To convert it to a percentage, multiply by 100.

Examples: The following calculates the interest rate (#40) based on a present value of $100,000 (#10), a payment amount of $1,000 per month (#20) over 20 years:

#40 = @IR(#10, #20, #30 * 12) * 100

The interest rate will be .877 % (note the multiplication by 100 to convert to a percentage).

@LEFT(Field, Number)

Program, Update, Navigation, Retrieve, Merge, Derived

Description: Returns Number of characters from the left side of Field.

Parameters:	**Field**—This should be an expression.
	Number—This should be an expression that results in a number. It represents the number of characters to return from the left.
Notes:	This programing function can be abbreviated as @LT. All of the parameters remain the same.
	If the Number is 0 then a blank value is returned.
Examples:	In a Retrieve Spec:
	{ @LEFT(First Name, 1) = @LEFT(Last Name, 1) }
	Retrieves all records where the First Name and Last Names begin with the same initial, such as Ronald Reagan, King Kong, and Billy Budd.
See Also:	*@RIGHT* to return the rightmost characters from a field.

@LEN(Field)

Program, Update, Navigation, Retrieve, Merge, Derived

Description:	Returns a number representing the length (in characters) of Field. If Field is blank, then @LEN returns 0.
Parameters:	**Field**—This should be an expression of which you want to find the length.
Notes:	Even if the text in a field extends beyond the size of the field and into the Field Editor, @LEN will return the length of the total field.
Examples:	In a Retrieve Spec:
	{ @LEN(First Name) = @LEN(Last Name) }
	Retrieves records where the length of the First Name is the same as the length of the Last Name, such as Jon Doe, Dave Reid, and William Johnson.
See Also:	*@WIDTH* to return the size of a field regardless of the length of the text in the field.

Lookup Functions and Statements _____

Program, Update, Navigation, Retrieve, Merge, Derived

@LOOKUP(Key, Column)

LOOKUP(Key, Column Field)

@LOOKUPR(Key, Column)

LOOKUPR(Key, Column, Field)

Description: Retrieves a value from Column from the database's built-in Lookup Table. The value retrieved is based on Key matching the key column of the Lookup Table. The LOOKUPR statement and @LOOKUPR function will retrieve the next lowest value if Key does not exist. The LOOKUP and LOOKUPR statements place the retrieved value in Field (if Key does not exist, then Field is left unchanged), as opposed to @LOOKUP and @LOOKUPR which return the retrieved value (if Key does not exist, then a blank value is returned).

Parameters: **Key**—This is an expression which should evaluate to the value to "look up" in the Lookup Table.

   Column—This is an expression which should evaluate to the number of the column containing the information to retrieve.

   Field—(LOOKUP and LOOKUPR only) This is an expression which should evaluate to the Field ID, or Field Name in which to place the value retrieved.

Notes: LOOKUP can be abbreviated as LU. LOOKUPR can be abbreviated as LUR. @LOOKUP can be abbreviated as @LU. @LOOKUPR can be abbreviated as @LUR. The parameters remain the same.

Examples: In a Mail Merge Document:

```
...your free gift is *PG {@LOOKUP(Gift
Code, 1)}...
```

   Would lookup up the text value found in the Gift Code field in the Key Column of the Lookup Table, and would return the corresponding data in column 1.

If you want to determine the zodiac sign of a person based on their birthday, you can create date ranges which correspond to the appropriate sign. The following is a sample of what the Lookup Table might look like:

KEY	1	2	3
03/21	Aries		
04/20	Taurus		
05/21	Gemini		
etc...			

This would create the following ranges:

Date Range	Sign
March 21 - April 19	Aries
April 20 - May 20	Taurus
May 21 - June 20	Gemini
etc...	

The statement to use this table follows:

```
LOOKUPR(@STR(@RIGHT(Birthday,5)),1,Sign)
```

For example, if the Birthday field is May 13, 1961, then the first part of the statement extracts the month and the day (i.e., 05/13). When no match is found for 05/13, the next lowest value is searched for. This would result in 04/20 being found. Therefore, Sign would contain the text string "Taurus."

See Also: *Edit Lookup Table* in the File Chapter for information on the database's built-in Lookup Table.

@RIGHT for information on extracting text from the right side of a string.

@LOOKUP(Key, Column)

See *Lookup Functions and Statements*

LOOKUP(Key, Column, Field)

See *Lookup Functions and Statements*

@LOOKUPR(Key, Column) _____

See *Lookup Functions and Statements*

LOOKUPR(Key, Column, Field) _____

See *Lookup Functions and Statements*

@MAX(List) _____

Program, Update, Navigation, Retrieve, Merge, Derived

Description: Calculates the maximum of the nonblank values in the List.

Parameters: **List**—This is a comma-delimited (i.e., separated by commas) list of expressions. A range of Field IDs (e.g., #10, #11, #12, and so on through #20) may be represented with two periods between the lowest and highest Field IDs (e.g., #10..#20). A range of Field Names that differ due only to a unique number at the end of the name (e.g., Test1, Test2, Test3, and so on through Test10), may also be separated by two periods and included in the list (e.g., Test1..Test10).

Notes: This function can be abbreviated as @MX. The parameter remains the same.

Examples: To find the slowest time of three different heats (fields ids are #10 through #30) for a runner in the 100-yard dash:

```
Slowest Time = @MX(#10, #20, #30)
```

@MID(Field, Start Position, Number) _____

Program, Update, Navigation, Retrieve, Merge, Derived

Description: Returns Number characters of Field starting from Start Position.

Parameters: **Field**—This should be an expression representing the text from which you want to return some characters from the middle.

Start Position—This should be an expression that results in a number. It represents the position of the first character in Field to return.

Number—This can be an expression that results in a number. It represents the number of characters to return.

Notes: This programing function can be abbreviated as @MD. All of the parameters remain the same.

If Start Position is less than or equal to 0 then the return value will start with the first character of Field. If Start Position is a number greater than the length of Field then no value will be returned.

If Number is less than or equal to 0 then no value will be returned.

Examples: In a Derived Column:

`@MID( Phone Number, 5, 8)`

If Phone Number has entries formatted as 123-456-7890, this function creates a Derived Column with just the prefix and suffix portions of a phone number, excluding the area code and any extensions.

_____ *@MIN(List)*

Program, Update, Navigation, Retrieve, Merge, Derived

Description: Calculates the minimum of the nonblank values in the List.

Parameters: **List**—This is a comma-delimited (i.e., separated by commas) list of expressions. A range of Field IDs (e.g., #10, #11, #12, and so on through #20) may be represented with two periods between the lowest and highest Field IDs (e.g., #10..#20). A range of Field Names that differ due only to a unique number at the end of the name (e.g., Test1, Test2, Test3, and so on through Test10), may also be separated by two periods and included in the list (e.g., Test1..Test10).

Notes: This function can be abbreviated as @MN. The parameter remains the same.

Examples: To find the first contact date with a customer, from three different contact times:

```
First Contact = @MIN(Call1, Call2,
Call3)
```

@MOD(Number, Modulo) _____

Program, Update, Navigation, Retrieve, Merge, Derived

Description: Calculates the smallest nonnegative integer when Modulo is repeatedly added to make a negative Number positive, or subtracted to minimize a positive Number.

Parameters: **Number**—This is an expression that should evaluate to a numeric value whose modulus is taken.

                  Modulo—This is an expression that should evaluate to a numeric value used as the modulus.

Notes: This function can be abbreviated as @MD. All parameters remain the same.

                  The modulus where both Number and Modulo are positive values is just the remainder of the Number divided by the Modulo. If the Modulo is 0, then the return value is 0.

@MONTH(Date) _____

Program, Update, Navigation, Retrieve, Merge, Derived

Description: Returns a number representing the month of Date.

Parameters: **Date**—This is any expression that evaluates to a date.

Notes: This programing function can be abbreviated as @MT. All of the parameters remain the same.

Examples: @MONTH("July, 4, 1776")

                  This function returns the number 7 because July is the seventh month of the year.

See Also: *@MONTH$* to return the name of a month.

_____ *@MONTH$(Date)*

Program, Update, Navigation, Retrieve, Merge, Derived

Description: Returns the name of the month of Date.

Parameters: **Date**—This is any expression that evaluates to a date.

Notes: This programing function can be abbreviated as @MT$. All of the parameters remain the same.

Examples: In a Retrieve Spec:

Birthdate: { @MONTH$(Birthdate) = "January" }

Retrieves all records on which birthdate is in the month of January.

See Also: *@MONTH* to return the number of a month.

_____ *@MSG(Message)*

Program, Navigation

Description: Displays the text of Message highlighted on the line above the function key line.

Parameters: **Message**—This should be an expression resulting in a text string. Only 80 characters can be displayed, so any text beyond 80 characters will not be displayed.

Notes: @MSG is a statement, not a function. Therefore, it does not return any value.

Examples: @MSG can be used to assist during data entry:

Department: < @MSG("Enter Sales, Finance, or Support")

As the user moves into the Department field, the specified message appears on the Message Line.

_____ *Multi-User Functions*

Description: The following functions return information on the current user of a secured database (i.e., with password protection or field level security):

@**GROUP**—Gets the name of the field security
group to which the current user belongs.

@**USERID**—Gets the User ID of the current user of
the database.

Navigation Statements

Description: These statements control movement of the cursor
during data entry. Upon entering or leaving a field,
they put the cursor at an exact location. The following are the available Navigation Statements:

CEND—Moves the cursor to the last field on the
record.

CHOME—Moves the cursor to the first field on
the record.

CNEXT—Moves the cursor to the next field on the
record.

CPREV—Moves the cursor to the previous field on
the record.

GOTO Field—Moves the cursor directly to Field
(Do not pass GO, do not collect $200). Field
must be a valid Field ID or Field Name.

PGDN—Moves the cursor to the first field on the
next page of the record.

PGUP—Moves the cursor to the first field on the
previous page of the record.

Notes: Navigation Statements can be entered only into fields
that are executed either On Field Entry or Exit.

@NUM(Field)

Program, Update, Navigation, Retrieve, Merge, Derived

Description: Returns a string containing only numeric characters
from Field. The numerals appear in their original order.

Parameters: **Field**—This should be an expression from which
you want to return the numeric characters.

Notes: The returned value is treated as a text value.

Examples: @NUM("123 Main Street, Apt 4B")

Returns the string "1234".

_____ *@NUMBER(Number)*

Program, Update, Navigation, Initial

Description: Returns a number that is Number units greater than the last time @NUMBER was executed.

Parameters: **Number**—This should be an expression that results in a number. It can also be 0 or negative.

Notes: This programming function can be abbreviated as @NMB. All of the parameters remain the same.

This parameter Number is optional. If it is excluded, @NUMBER returns the same values as @NUMBER(1).

On the Initial Values Spec, you may not include the Number parameter.

You may reset the value of @NUMBER from Add Data or Search/Update. To reset the value, press Ctrl-F8 from Add Data or Search/Update, type a number that is Number less than the next return you want from @NUMBER (e.g., if you want @NUMBER to start with 1, reset the number to 0, or if you want @NUMBER(10) to start with 1000, reset the number to 990).

Examples: On the Initial Values Spec:

Invoice Number: @NUMBER

numbers each Invoice sequentially.

To give ID numbers to new customers that are in increments of 100, use the following statement:

Customer Number: #1 = @NUMBER(100)

_____ *PGDN*

See *Navigation Statements*

PGUP _____

See *Navigation Statements*

@PMT(Present Value, Interest, Number of Payments) _____

Program, Update, Navigation, Retrieve, Merge, Derived

Description: Calculates the payment amount of a loan based on Present Value, Interest, and Number of Payments.

Parameters: **Present Value**—This is an expression that should evaluate to the amount of the loan left to pay.

   Interest—This is an expression that should evaluate to the interest rate per payment. This value must be greater than or equal to –1, and expressed as a decimal value. To convert it to a decimal, divide by 100.

   Number of Payments—This is an expression that should evaluate to the number of payments made for the investment.

Notes: The formula that Q&A uses to calculate the payments is:

```
PMT = Present * Interest / 1 - (1 + In-
terest) ^ (- Number of Payments)
```

Examples: The following will calculate the payment amount (#40) for a loan with a repayment amount of $10,000 (#10) over a 10-year period (#30) at 2% interest per month (#20):

```
#40 = @PMT(#10, #20 / 100, #30 * 12)
```

The payment amount will be $220.48 per month.

Program Editor _____

See *Field Editor* in the File Chapter for information about editing programming statements beyond the length of a single field.

@PV(Payment Amount, Interest, Number of Payments)

Program, Update, Navigation, Retrieve, Merge, Derived

Description: Calculates the present value of an investment based on Payment Amount, Interest, and Number of Payments.

Parameters: **Payment Amount**—This is an expression that should evaluate to the desired payment amount of the investment.

Interest—This is an expression that should evaluate to the interest rate per payment. This value must be greater than or equal to −1, and should be expressed as a decimal value. To convert it to a decimal value, divide by 100.

Number of Payments—This is an expression that should evaluate to the number of payments to make for the investment.

Notes: The formula that Q&A uses to calculate the present value is:

```
PV = Payment * ((1 - (1 + Interest) ^
(Number of Payments)) / Interest)
```

Examples: The following calculates the present value (#40) of an investment with $150 payments for a period of 10 years at a periodic interest rate of 5 percent:

```
#40 = @PV(150, 5 / 100, 10 * 12)
```

The present value will be $2991.40.

@REPLFIR(Field, Search, Replace)

See *@REPLACE*.

@REPLACE(Field, Search, Replace)

Program, Update, Navigation, Retrieve, Merge, Derived

Description: Replaces all occurrences of Search with Replace in Field. Two variations of this command are @REPLFIR and @REPLLAS. @REPLFIR replaces the first occur-

rence of Search with Replace in Field, and
@REPLLAS replaces the last occurrence of Search
with Replace in Field.

Parameters: **Field**—This should be an expression.

Search—This is the text that will be replaced. It
should be an expression that results in text.

Replace—This text will replace all occurrences of
the text from the Search parameter. It should
be an expression that results in text.

Notes: To remove all occurrences of something, replace it
with two quote marks with nothing between them
(*""*).

Examples: `Dimensions: #36 = @REPLACE( #36, "inch", "in")`

Replaces all occurrence of the word "inch" with the
abbreviation "in".

If your database contained standard legal paragraphs
using the term "defendant", you could replace all occurrences of "defendant" with the name of your
client using the following Merge Document Programming command:

`*Program {@REPLACE(Paragraph 1, "Defend-
ant", "Susan Beech") } *`

@REPLLAS(Field, Search, Replace) _____

See **@REPLACE**.

@REST(Field, Restriction) _____

Program, Update, Navigation, Retrieve, Merge, Derived

Description: Returns a YES or NO value based on the value of
Field meeting the conditions of Restriction. If Field
meets the conditions placed by Restriction, then the
return value will be YES, otherwise it will be NO.

Parameters:	**Field**—This is an expression that evaluates to the Field ID, or Field Name to restrict.
	Restriction—This is an expression that evaluates to the text string representing the restriction to apply to Field. Any restriction that is valid on a Retrieve Spec may be used here, including those containing programming.
Examples:	To determine if a temperature is Above Zero:

```
Above Zero: Above Zero =
@REST(Temperature, "> 0")
```

This will determine if the value in the Temperature field is greater than 0 (i.e., "> 0"), and will return YES if this condition is met, and NO otherwise.

See Also: *Retrieve Spec* in the File Chapter for a list of valid restrictions.

_____ *RETURN*

Program

Description: Ends a programming subroutine by returning program control back to the field that began the subroutine with a GOSUB command. Programming execution will continue with those statements immediately following the GOSUB command.

Notes: RETURN commands can be entered only into fields that are On Field Entry.

Examples: See the GOSUB command for an example of how RETURN is used to create subroutines.

See Also: *GOSUB* for information about the command that begins a subroutine.

_____ *@RIGHT(Field, Number)*

Program, Update, Navigation, Retrieve, Merge, Derived

Description: Returns Number characters from the right side of Field.

Parameters:	**Field**—This should be an expression.
	Number—This should be an expression that results in a number. It represents the number of characters to return from the right of Field.
Notes:	This programing function can be abbreviated as @RT. All of the parameters remain the same.
	If the Number is 0 then a blank value is returned.
Examples:	`Customer Number: #3 = @Right( Phone Number, 4)`
	Assigns the last four characters from the Phone Number field as the Customer Number.
See Also:	*@LEFT* to return the leftmost characters from a field.

@ROUND(Number, Decimal) _____

Program, Update, Navigation, Retrieve, Merge, Derived

Description:	Rounds Number to Decimal digits past the decimal point.
Parameters:	**Number**—This is an expression that evaluates to the numeric value to round.
	Decimal—This is an expression that evaluates to a numeric value representing the number of decimal digits used to round the Number. If this expression evaluates to a noninteger number, the value will be rounded down, and then used. This value must be in the range from –15 to 15.
Notes:	This function can be abbreviated as @RND. The parameters remain the same.
Examples:	`#10 = @ROUND(minutes/60,2) * 100`
	This will calculate the number of minutes that have elapsed as a percentage of an hour.
	`#10 = @ROUND(Monthly Sales, -3)`
	This will round the value of the Monthly Sales to the nearest 1000 dollars (e.g., if Monthly Sales are $234,567 then this statement will assign to #10 the value $235,000).

@SELECT(Number, Item 1, Item 2, ...)

Program, Update, Navigation, Retrieve, Merge, Derived

Description: Returns the element from the list of Items corresponding to Number.

Parameters: **Number**—This should be an expression resulting in a number.

Items—There must at least two Items. These will often be text strings, but may be any expression. The values returned by @SELECT will be text, regardless of the type of the Item in the list.

Notes: If the Number parameter is greater than the number of Items in the list, then the last Item is returned. If the Number is 0 or negative, the last item is also returned.

If the Number is not an integer, the integer portion of it is used as the selector.

Examples: To assign a Region Name with only a number, and also to catch errors in entry:

```
Region Code: >Region Name = @Select( Re-
gion Code, "Western", "Central", "East-
ern", "Invalid Selection")
```

If the number 1, 2, or 3 is entered, the corresponding Region Name is returned. If a number is entered that is less than 1 or greater than or equal to 4, the fourth Item in the list will be returned.

@SGN(Number)

Program, Update, Navigation, Retrieve, Merge, Derived

Description: Returns a value representing the sign of Number.

Parameters: **Number**—This is an expression that evaluates to a numeric value.

Notes: This function returns a 0 if Number equals 0, 1 if Number is positive (i.e., greater than 0), and −1 if Number is negative (i.e., less than 0).

Examples: To find the sign of the temperature:

`#10: IF @SGN(Temp) > 0 THEN Above Zero =`
`"TRUE" ELSE Above Zero = "FALSE"`

@SQRT(Number)

Program, Update, Navigation, Retrieve, Merge, Derived

Description: Returns the square root of Number.

Parameters: **Number**—This is an expression that should evaluate to a numeric value to square root. If the
number is less than zero, then the function
takes the square root of the absolute value of
the number.

Notes: This function can be abbreviated as @SQ. The parameter remains the same.

Examples: The following statement calculates the square root
of 9:

`#10 = @SQRT(9)`

@STD(List)

Program, Update, Navigation, Retrieve, Merge, Derived

Description: Calculates the standard deviation of the nonblank
values in List.

Parameters: **List**—This is a comma-delimited (i.e., separated by
commas) list of expressions that should evalu-
ate to numeric or monetary values. A range of
Field IDs (e.g., #10, #11, #12, and so on
through #20) may be represented with two periods between the lowest and highest Field IDs
(e.g., #10..#20). A range of Field Names that
differ due only to a unique number at the end
of the name (e.g., Test1, Test2, Test3, and so on
through Test10), may also be separated by two
periods and included in the list (e.g.,
Test1..Test10).

Notes: The standard deviation is the square root of the variance of a list of expressions.

Examples: To calculate the standard deviation of a list of 5 test scores (the fields Test1 through Test5 are labeled #10 through #50):

#100 = @STD(#10..#50)

_____ *STOP*

Program

Description: This command stops all program execution. The cursor is left in the field containing the STOP command. If STOP is executed in a GOSUB subroutine, all pending RETURN statements are canceled.

Examples: Region: > IF Region <> "Western" THEN
STOP

This statement STOPs all programming if the region does not equal "Western".

See Also: *GOSUB* for more information about GOSUB subroutines.

RETURN for more information about the RETURN command.

_____ *@STR(Value)*

See *Typecasting Functions.*

_____ *@SUM(List)*

Program, Update, Navigation, Retrieve, Merge, Derived

Description: Finds the sum of the nonblank values in List.

Parameters: List—This is a comma-delimited (i.e., separated by commas) list of expressions that should evaluate to numeric or monetary values. A range of Field IDs (e.g., #10, #11, #12, and so on through #20) may be represented with two periods between the lowest and highest Field IDs (e.g., #10..#20). A range of Field Names that differ due only to a unique number at the end of the name (e.g., Test1, Test2, Test3, and so on through Test10), may also be separated by two periods and included in the list (e.g., Test1..Test10).

Examples: To total the monthly sales for the year 1991 if the monthly sales are numbered #10 through #120:

`Total = @SUM(#10..#120)`

@TEXT(Number, String) _____

Program, Update, Navigation, Retrieve, Merge, Derived

Description: Returns Number copies of String. These copies of String are concatenated together.

Parameters: **Number**—This should be an expression resulting in a number. If the Number is 0 then @TEXT returns a blank value.

String—This is an expression resulting in a text string that @TEXT will return Number times.

Notes: This programing function can be abbreviated as @TXT. All of the parameters remain the same.

Examples: `@TEXT( 3, "abc")`

Returns three copies of ''abc'', or ''abcabcabc''.

@TIME _____

Program, Update, Navigation, Retrieve, Merge, Derived, Initial

Description: Returns the current time from the system clock.

Notes: This programing function can be abbreviated as @TME.

If the system clock is not accurate, then @TIME will return an incorrect time.

Examples: `Status: IF @TIME > 5pm THEN Status = "Ov-erdue"`

If the current time is past 5 p.m., then the Status field is marked overdue.

See Also: *@DATE* to return the current date from the system clock.

_____ *@TODATE(Value)*

See *Typecasting Functions.*

_____ *@TOMONEY(Value)*

See *Typecasting Functions.*

_____ *@TONUMBER(Value)*

See *Typecasting Functions.*

_____ *@TOTIME(Value)*

See *Typecasting Functions.*

_____ *@TOYESNO(Value)*

See *Typecasting Functions.*

_____ *Typecasting Functions*

Description: The following functions convert expressions from one
data type to another:

> **@STR(expression)**—Converts an expression of any
> type to a text value.

> **@TODATE(expression)**—Converts an expression
> of either text or keyword type to a date value.
> If the expression cannot be converted, a blank
> value will be returned. This function can be ab-
> breviated as @TD.

> **@TONUMBER(expression)**—Converts an expres-
> sion of any type to a numeric value. Money
> types are converted to their numeric equivalent,
> and Text and Keyword types are stripped of all
> non-numeric characters. Date types are con-
> verted as the number of days elapsed since 1/
> 1/1. Time types are converted as the number

of minutes elapsed since 12:00 a.m. Yes/No types are converted as 1 for Yes and 0 for No. This function can be abbreviated as @TN.

@TOMONEY(expression)—Converts an expression of any type to a monetary value. Numeric types are converted to their monetary equivalent and all other types are first converted to their numeric equivalent and then to a monetary value. This function can be abbreviated as @TM.

@TOTIME(expression)—Converts an expression of a text, or keyword type to a time value. If the expression cannot be converted, a blank value will be returned. This function can be abbreviated as @TT.

@TOYESNO(expression)—Converts an expression of any type to a Boolean (i.e., Yes/No, or True/False) value. Text and Keyword types return Yes if the value is 1, T, TRUE, Y, or Yes; any other value returns No. Numeric and Monetary types return Yes if the value is 1, or $1.00; any other value returns No. Date and Time types always return No.

@UPDATE

See *Context Functions*

@USERID

See *Multi-User Functions.*

@VAR(List)

Program, Update, Navigation, Retrieve, Merge, Derived

Description: Finds the variance of the nonblank values in List.

Parameters: **List**—This is a comma-delimited (i.e., separated by commas) list of expressions that should evaluate to numeric or monetary values. A range of

Field IDs (e.g., #10, #11, #12, and so on through #20) may be represented with two periods between the lowest and highest Field IDs (e.g., #10..#20). A range of Field Names that differ due only to a unique number at the end of the name (e.g., Test1, Test2, Test3, and so on through Test10), may also be separated by two periods and included in the list (e.g., Test1..Test10).

Examples: To calculate the variance of 5 test score fields, Test1 through Test5, labeled #10 through #50:

`#100 = @VAR(#10..#50)`

@WIDTH(Field ID)

Program, Update, Navigation, Retrieve, Merge, Derived

Description: Returns a number representing the size in characters of the Field ID as it appears on the screen.

Parameters: **Field ID**—This must be a valid Field ID or Field Name.

Notes: This programing function can be abbreviated as @WTH. All of the parameters remain the same.

Even if the text in Field ID extends beyond the size of the Field ID and into the Field Editor, @WIDTH will return the size of just the Field itself.

Examples: To return only those characters that fit into a Comments field on the screen:

`Comments = @LEFT( Comments, @WIDTH( Comments ) )`

See Also: *@LEN* to return the length of a field regardless of whether it extends into the Field Editor or not.

Xlookup Functions and Statements

Program, Update, Navigation, Retrieve, Merge, Derived

@XLOOKUP(Filename, Key, External Key, Lookup Field)

XLOOKUP(Filename, Key, External Key, Lookup Field, Field)

@XLOOKUPR(Filename, Key, External Key, Lookup Field)

XLOOKUPR(Filename, Key, External Key, Lookup Field, Field)

Description: These statements and functions retrieve the value of Lookup Field from the database specified by Filename. The value retrieved is based on a match of Key with the External Key field in the external database. The XLOOKUPR statement and @XLOOKUPR function will retrieve the record with the next lowest value if an exact match is not found. XLOOKUP and XLOOKUPR place the retrieved value in Field (if no record is retrieved, the Field value is left unchanged), as opposed to the @XLOOKUP and @XLOOKUPR, which return the retrieved value (if no record is retrieved, a blank value is returned).

Parameters: **Filename**—This is an expression that should evaluate to the path and name of the external database to search. If no path is used, the default database path specified in the *Set Global Options* command of the Utilities Chapter is used.

Key—This is an expression that should evaluate to the value to "look up" in the external database.

External Key—This is an expression that should evaluate to the Field ID or Field Name of the external field in which to search to find a match for Key. This field must be an indexed field.

Lookup Field—This is an expression that should evaluate to the Field ID or Field Name of the external field from which to retrieve the data when a match is found.

Field—(XLOOKUP and XLOOKUPR only) This is an expression that should evaluate to the Field ID or Field Name in the current database in which to place the value retrieved.

Notes: XLOOKUP can be abbreviated as XLU. XLOOKUPR can be abbreviated as XLR. @XLOOKUP can be abbreviated as @XLU. @XLOOKUPR can be abbreviated as @XLR. All parameters remain the same.

A single XLOOKUP or XLOOKUPR statement can retrieve multiple values to place in corresponding fields in the current database. The syntax is as follows:

XLOOKUP(Filename, Key, External Key, Lookup Field 1, Field 1, Lookup Field 2, Field 2, ..., Lookup Field 23, Field 23)

The statement works exactly as described above, however, more information can be retrieved with a single statement.

These statements can also retrieve information from dBase databases using the same parameters.

Examples: In a Mass Update, on the Update Spec:

```
XLOOKUP("CLIENTS.DTF", Client ID, "X#10",
"X#20", Contact, "X#30", Contact Phone)
```

would update each record in an invoice database by following these steps:

1. Find a record in the external database in which the External Key field #10 (this is the field number found in Program Form of the CLIENTS.DTF database) matches the Client ID of the current record.

2. If step 1 is successful, then from the record found in the external database, extract the values in the Lookup Fields #20 and #30 (these are the field numbers found in Program Form of the CLIENTS.DTF database) and place them in the Contact and Contact Phone fields respectively of the current record. If step 1 is unsuccessful (i.e., no record is found in the external database), then leave the values of the Contact and Contact Phone fields unchanged.

See Also: *Speed Up Searches* in the File Chapter for information on indexing a field.

Set Global Options in the Utilities Chapter for information on specifying the default database path.

@XLOOKUP(Filename, Key, External Key, Lookup Field)

See *Xlookup Functions and Statements*

XLOOKUP(Filename, Key, External Key, Lookup Field, Field) _____

See *Xlookup Functions and Statements*

@XLOOKUPR(Filename, Key, External Key, Lookup Field) _____

See *Xlookup Functions and Statements*

XLOOKUPR(Filename, Key, External Key, Lookup Field, Field) _____

See *Xlookup Functions and Statements*

@YEAR(Date) _____

Program, Update, Navigation, Retrieve, Merge, Derived

Description: Returns a four-digit number representing the year of Date.

Parameters: **Date**—This is any expression that evaluates to a date.

Notes: This programming function can be abbreviated as @YR. All of the parameters remain the same.

Examples: @YEAR(@DATE)-@YEAR("July 4, 1776")

Returns the number of years since the signing of the Declaration of Independence.

Index